SBERBANK
The Rebirth of Russia's Financial Giant

Glagoslav Publications

SBERBANK
THE REBIRTH OF RUSSIA'S FINANCIAL GIANT

by Evgeny Karasyuk

© 2014, Evgeny Karasyuk

Translated by Lewis White

Edited by James Womack

Cover design by Kiryl Lysenka

© 2015, Glagoslav Publications, United Kingdom

Glagoslav Publications Ltd
88-90 Hatton Garden
EC1N 8PN London
United Kingdom

www.glagoslav.com

ISBN: 978-1-78267-091-9

This book is in copyright. No part of this publication may be reproduced, stored in a retrieval system or transmitted in any form or by any means without the prior permission in writing of the publisher, nor be otherwise circulated in any form of binding or cover other than that in which it is published without a similar condition, including this condition, being imposed on the subsequent purchaser.

CONTENTS

Preface 4

Chapter 1. INSOMNIA 7

Chapter 2. THE MAIN STRATEGIST 22

Chapter 3. STRANGE THINGS 34

Chapter 4. A PRISON FOR MONEY 44

Chapter 5. COMMON SENSE IS ALWAYS WRONG 53

Chapter 6. I KNEW NOTHING ABOUT LEAN 60

Chapter 7. THE 5S DEEP CLEAN 79

Chapter 8. THE CREATIVE CLASS 89

Chapter 9. NO MORE DOING THE SLIPS! 94

Chapter 10. THE BILLION-DOLLAR SWINDLE 102

Chapter 11. I'LL BE MAKING A COMPLAINT 111

Chapter 12. DENIAL, ANGER, BARGAINING, DEPRESSION AND ACCEPTANCE 125

Chapter 13. COUNTING SHARES ON ONE HAND 137

Chapter 14. SPARE PEOPLE 147

Chapter 15. AN UNLUCKY NUMBER 158

Chapter 16. "OUT OF THE BLUE" 167

Chapter 17. KICKING CLIENTS WHEN THEY'RE DOWN? 175

Chapter 18. MORE THAN A BANK 188

Chapter 19. BUYING TIME 199

Chapter 20. ISN'T IT JUST US? 210

Acknowledgements 221

Notes 223

PREFACE

THE AUTUMN OF 2007 WAS AN UNUSUALLY WARM ONE. Many said that such high temperatures hadn't been recorded in central Russia since the end of the 19th century. Fallen leaves mouldered underfoot, but the sun blazed above as if it were the height of summer. Paying no heed to the calendar, most Muscovites went about their business without the heavy clothing characteristic of the season.

Those at the head office of Russia's largest bank found themselves unable to make the most of the unseasonably good weather. They were not much in the mood. Everyone was too preoccupied with the arrival of the new boss — transfers of power in big organisations do not always work out for the better.

The big organisation in question was Sberbank. The incoming boss was German Gref. Much was known about him, but little of it was encouraging. In his previous post as government minister he had been an irrepressible reformer, earning a reputation as a systematic liberaliser of the economy, the choicest cuts of which were controlled by the state and the handful of business figures close to it. This kind of man was easy to imagine in business — but on the board of some transnational corporation, not Sberbank.

The largest bank in the country was a virtual monopoly, albeit not in the strictest sense of the word. Among commercial banks it was known as the Ministry of Deposits. Sberbank looked down imperiously on the rest of the market, and was no more inclined to change than Gazprom, Russian Railways, Russian Post, or any other hulking state behemoth. So where did this spirit of reform emerge from?

For ordinary companies it requires a tremendous effort for things to go from worse to bad, and then to good only if luck is on their side. Reform is a fundamental condition of their survival. There's always the potential for the money to run out, and creditors circle like vultures. Competitors champ at the bit to muscle in, and regulators offer no quarter. In truth, major reforms in business are rarely brought about by anything other than desparation. But Sberbank didn't share anything in common with these unfortunates; its existence was remarkable for its uneventfulness and predictability. The regulator moonlighted as its main shareholder. Strong binoculars were required to spot the competition, they were so far behind. As for money, the bank was flush, and has only got richer in recent times.

Market capitalisation in the middle of 2007 exceeded $86 billion: in Russia Sberbank was trumped only by Gazprom in this regard. Its market valuation outstripped that of major European banking concerns such as Commerzbank and Deutsche Bank. As for the figures it posted, these were beyond reproach; stable results with good revenue and interest earnings garnered the plaudits of analysts year after year. The state bank team was regarded as a model in the idiosyncratic world of the post-Soviet financial *nomenklatura*. The head of the banking subcommittee of the Russian State Duma, Pavel Medvedev, and ex-member of the Sberbank supervisory board, Anton Danilov-Danilyan, stated that the company was run by a "top-grade manager" and a "brilliant banker". The management was showered with professional awards from top-ranking financial officials with effusive expressions of their gratitude.

This corporate idyll was only spoiled by one thing: Sberbank was not much loved by its customers. In this sense it brought to mind the country it served. Behind the government's official crowing lay a rather more grim reality: that many citizens of such an enormous, resource-rich state led an abject existence.

Despite "the brilliance of the bankers", its customers found dealing with Sberbank a tortuous ordeal. International research agency EPSI, who regularly gauged client satisfaction with Russian banks, reported that Sberbank was in protracted crisis. But until the baking autumn of 2007 this was not seen as much of a problem. Who had time for such trivialities when there were growing profits and stock prices to celebrate?

Enter German Gref, ex-minister, liberal, and tireless reformer. Sberbank staff had been right in their misgivings. The new boss was the kind of oddity that cared about what his customers thought. This most venerable of banking instutions, sure in its inviolability, faced an overhaul the likes of which it had never seen in all of its long history.

Chapter 1
INSOMNIA

BELLA ZLATKIS COULDN'T SLEEP. THIS WASN'T LIKE her at all. No matter what was happening at work, her nervous system was configured so that she was usually asleep before her head touched the pillow. But not tonight. Zlatkis sat in the kitchen absorbed with thoughts of the coming day. She smoked one cigarette and unconsciously reached for the next. In the last few hours, Zlatkis had taken in more nicotine than over the entire previous month.

A session of the Sberbank supervisory board — or, to put it another way, the board of directors of the most powerful financial institution in the land, responsible for the savings of a good half of the population — had been called for the following morning. Zlatkis had taken part in similar meetings for years as a Finance Ministry official. In professional circles she was regarded as something of a legend, one of the most experienced experts on financial markets. Consequently, when in 2004 she had transferred from the Ministry to Sberbank, her new superior, Andrei Kazmin, had rushed to get her back where she belonged. Kazmin supported her candidacy and she reappeared on the supervisory board, this time as a representative of the bank's management. At this point, no-one could have predicted that wrangling at the top would later force Zlatkis to make what was possibly the most difficult moral choice of her life.

> "The stable position of the bank in the retail market is guaranteed not only by its multiple branches, its working traditions and impeccable business reputation, but by the high standard of service it offers the population."
>
> From the introductory section of the anniversary booklet *"Sberbank Rossii: Istoriya, Sovremennost', Perspektivy"* (2001).

The current board was preparing to oust Kazmin, head of Sberbank for almost 12 years, and appoint as his successor German Gref, the former minister for economic trade and development.

Zlatkis had long enjoyed good relations with Kazmin, who was also a product of the finance ministry. She had known him for 17 years, and at the outset of his career had even been his boss for a period of time. Good-natured, pleasant-mannered, and intelligent, Kazmin spoke three languages, possessed a Master's degree and was soundly versed in economic theory. He was, however, let down by a dreadfully indecisive character — colleagues did not regard him as a natural leader, and Zlatkis, if pressed, would be forced to admit this herself.

Gref was made of different stuff. He always strove to master any situation, regardless of the circumstances. Of course, Gref was no banker. Until 2007, his entire banking experience could be considered incidental. In his ministerial capacity he had represented Russia on the board of the EBRD. He had sat on the Sberbank supervisory board for all of two and half years — that is, he'd been to around two dozen meetings. This didn't constitute much. Among professionals, Gref was an outsider. All his predecessors had built their careers at Sberbank, or had moved in the same circles. Kazmin had worked as an economist in one of the Moscow departments of Gosbank (which, at that time, operated a network of Soviet savings bank branches). Gref, on the other hand, had no education in economics, and as a result, became a regular object of his colleagues' sarcasm. Professional bankers were often less than respectful in their attitude towards him. They were sure that the minister had no idea what he'd let himself in for. Knowing the weakness

Viktor Gerashchenko, former head of the Central Bank, had for plain speaking, journalists badgered him for his thoughts, and he duly obliged: replacing Kazmin with Gref could turn out to be a foolish move.

Zlatkis didn't think so. She had known Gref even before he'd taken up the job of federal minister. To her, he was a man with progressive ideas and, no less importantly, a man of principles that hadn't been shaken by years in a government no steadier than the price of a barrel of oil. Gref continued to believe in the market, in competition, and in management as the science of transforming what needed doing into what had been done — just imagine what this could mean for Sberbank.

Dawn approached, but Zlatkis couldn't rest — it looked likely she'd end up among the opponents of Gref's appointment as head of the bank, whether she liked it or not. Zlatkis believed that she had no moral authority to vote any other way than as directed by her boss, and it didn't take much to guess what that meant.

Her last chance to avoid this undesirable course of events was to catch Kazmin before the meeting began. Zlatkis arrived for work early. The towering headquarters on Vavilov Street in south Moscow was just beginning to come to life for the day. Two and a half thousand employees had yet to make it to their desks, hidden in the depths of this wonder of post-Soviet banking architecture.

The decision to build Sberbank's new headquarters had been taken in the early nineties by Pavel Zhikharev, who had been in charge since the final days of the Soviet Union. He later complained that he had been tricked by Moscow mayor Yuri Luzhkov, who had allotted an unattractive location close to a power station, leading Zhikharev to believe that the plant would soon be shifted further from the centre. This move never took place, and billowing chimneys still spoil the view from east-facing windows. The scale of the project compensated somewhat for the rather unedifying surroundings. The skyscraper, made from smoked glass and white granite imported at eye-watering expense from South America, was constructed by a German firm of architects. Oleg Yashin, who had replaced Zhikharev, allotted himself the top floor of the building, which he had designed as a spacious retreat. However, Yashin didn't get much opportunity to enjoy his comfortable new office — in January 1996, immediately after the building was handed over following completion, he was dismissed (though Yashin only finally left the bank in October 1996, after just under two years advising the new president). After that, the coveted 25th floor was occupied by Andrei Kazmin and his partner Alla Aleshkina, who was also senior vice-president at the bank.

Zlatkis pressed the top button of the express elevator. She had hoped to speak to the president face to face, and she was in luck: Kazmin was alone. Judging by his expression, he hadn't slept particularly well the previous night either.

The president's sacking had long been augured. A motley crew of bankers and politicians had been tipped for Kazmin's desk, from former prime minister Sergei Kiriyenko to Vladimir Kogan, at that time head of Promstroibank, later sold to VTB. None of these wild predictions had been on the mark. Now, however, it seemed for real.

17 people sat on the supervisory board. Sberbank had just short of 237,000 shareholders, but only one of these had any real say — the Central Bank, which

owned more than 60% of its voting shares. And it had been decided — Kazmin had to go. The new prime minister Viktor Zubkov had officially proposed (and Vladmir Putin had nothing against) sending Kazmin to take over at Russian Post, another gigantic state organisation. The transfer was worked out. The president of a limited company, even one controlled by the state, is not a state employee and cannot simply be sent anywhere on the say-so of the government. However, such minor details were not considered an issue — a space at the post office had been cleared for him, and its unsuspecting general director Igor Syrtsov unceremoniously shown the door.

In turn, Gref's appointment as president of the bank would be up for discussion at the supervisory board, and at an extraordinary meeting of shareholders, but only for form's sake; expressions of dissent at his candidacy were empty gestures.

Zlatkis immediately made it clear that she didn't regard any parting shots from Kazmin a good idea. Sberbank was the culmination of his career, but not the end of it. Arguing against the state's choice at a state bank? What was the use? The president was not ready to be lectured that morning, but he might allow himself to be persuaded. Perhaps Kazmin recognised that supporting a successor recommended by the main shareholder would be taken as a display of loyalty — loyalty to an employer upon whom his destiny might later depend.

However, such efforts became academic with the arrival on the scene of his other half, whose word he hung on in all major issues, and who had no intention of going quietly. Alla Aleshkina loved power and hated anything that undermined her. Her presence had loomed over the bank for years. It was thanks to her that the inherent bureaucracy of the system had been perfected. Memoranda had all but replaced face-to-face contact between levels of the hierarchy, and everyone knew his or her place. Kazmin himself probably regarded his role as equivalent to being the referee of some rugby match, a sport he adored so much that he was prepared to travel the globe from Sydney to Paris so as not to miss the "fantastic spectacle". "In rugby it's not done for players to argue with the referee," Kazmin enthusiastically told an in-house magazine. "Only the team captain can speak to the referee and only with the referee's permission. The captain himself cannot approach the referee. The referee conducts the game with a radio relay. He has a transmitter and his entire team are audible to the crowd."

At first, Zlatkis had been surprised by the way things were done at the bank. She was used to the egalitarian atmosphere of the finance ministry: there, if something urgent needed to be discussed, it was normal to burst into the boss's office and have a heated exchange with him without having to bow and scrape. At Sberbank, this was utterly unthinkable. Zlatkis had been astounded to learn the degree of subordination a university friend of hers who worked at the bank was subjected to — there was even a silly bell that rang to indicate when to go to lunch.

The paradox lay in the fact that the atmosphere prevalent amongst the management approached hysteria. Personal dealings supplanted standardised systems of operation. People were constantly arguing, were not on speaking terms, or else avoided each other completely. Work would get bogged down in petty intrigues and pretences. Aleshkina could pull the plug on any senior manager she wasn't keen on, even if they weren't her direct subordinates.

Aleshkina's capriciousness was known beyond the confines of the bank. She would create a spectacular scene whenever some high-handed finance official needed to be dealt with. A couple of years previously, some unflattering appraisals of Sberbank's work following checks conducted by inspectors from the Central Bank had sent her into a furious rage, and, in protest, she boycotted meetings of the supervisory board, of which she, alongside Kazmin, had been a member.

The question of whether she'd dance to these upstarts' tune wasn't worth posing. Gref? How could a bank be trusted in the hands of an official with no banking experience? Aleshkina and her partner had been treated unfairly — monstrously, in fact. Who else if not them had brought the bank back from the brink?

In 1996 Kazmin and Aleshkina had taken on a failing bank that looked set to come apart at the seams at any moment. Feudal princes ruled in provincial territories, dishing out credit with scant regard to the risks. Sberbank had enormous problems with overdue loans and, consequently, liquidity. In some regions, such as Krasnoyarsk Krai, arrears had reached 97% of all loans in the local bank's portfolio. Among the bank's regional subdivisions it was normal not to share information on clients and any risks associated with them. It was an opportunist's dream. Small-scale commercial banks essentially functioned as corporate borrowers (at that time loans were not issued directly to businesses) and would amass tremendous amounts of credit in different regions with no intention of paying it back. Regulations that made it a requirement to coordinate with Moscow over the issuing of loans were flagrantly undermined. Regional managers knew full well that headquarters were wholly unable to monitor all their actions.

At that time, Zlatkis was heading up the securities and financial markets department at the finance ministry, and she was well aware of Sberbank's condition. "So much was pilfered that no-one knew how the bank was going to survive," she would say later.

However, the bank did survive. With state support, Kazmin and Aleshkina managed to steady the balance and even come out of the 1998 crisis relatively unscathed. Under them, the bank began to beef up its lending procedure, and over the course of a few years, the organisational structure of Sberbank was overhauled — the number of regional bank divisions was reduced from 71 at the outset to 17 in 2001, wiping out the feudal factionalism of before.

This staved off the threat of collapse. The International Monetary Fund, at that time an influential lender to Russia, proposed the breaking up of Sberbank into a number of individual parts shortly after August 1998. The IMF, concerned that a state monopoly was suffocating competition, advocated the revitalisation of the financial sector, and aimed to improve the governability of an organisation whose decision-making process had become overly complicated and lacked transparency.

Three quarters of the nation's savings were held by Sberbank — at that time the only Russian bank whose deposits were guaranteed by the state. As a result, the government was reluctant to follow the radical advice of the IMF experts. The government, the Central Bank and, naturally, the management itself, felt it best simply to integrate the internal sub-departments of the company. Subsequently, against a rise in the bank's profits and share price, Kazmin met all suggestions of restructuring with flat rejections. "In no country in the world would a rational government consider such a move", he bristled. "Why kill the goose that lays the golden eggs?"

By the 2000s the bank's management had begun peddling its successes like an election manifesto. In 2001 the main objective was not to capture hearts and minds, but "to preserve the position of a modern, first-rate, competitive bank, the largest in Eastern Europe." The results of the five-year development plan up to 2005 also painted a picture of untouchable dominance, boasting an assortment of unique competitive advantages, from the strong brand and reputation to its highly trained staff. Sberbank was one of the largest employers in the country, and recruited almost continually. More than 204,000 people worked for the bank in the period leading up to 2002, and six years later this number had exceeded 262,000. The size of its workforce was equivalent to the population of a small country such as Iceland or Barbados. With around 19,000 branches, the bank was second in the world for the scale of its branch network (the largest was that of the Industrial and Commercial Bank of China, with 37,000 branches, though this was later halved).

The market share of hundreds of other players was statistically negligible. Remove Sberbank from the equation, and the country's banking system would lose a quarter of its assets. In 2007, Sberbank's piece of the pie reached 5 trillion roubles. The quantity did not negate the quality. In the 1990s, three quarters of assets had been in securities, mostly in the infamous GKOs (Government Short-Term Commitments, bonds synonymous with the 1998 Russian financial crisis). Now their place had been taken by loans.

SBERBANK: THE REBIRTH OF RUSSIA'S FINANCIAL GIANT

> "In striving for perfection in banking, Sberbank devotes particular attention to optimising development paths based primarily on our clients' interests."
>
> Andrei Kazmin in the anniversary booklet *"Sberbank Rossii: Istoriya, Sovremennost', Perspektivy"* (2001).

The management was proud of the fact that it had transformed "a thrift institution system" into a commercial bank that "guaranteed a growth in profit returns of 25-30% yearly". The stock market looked on this with evident approval, and share prices rocketed — from 1998 the bank's market capitalisation grew 116 times, reaching $95.7 billion. This had all been down to Kazmin and Aleshkina.

The only thing missing to complete the picture was the love of its clients. The story of Sberbank's coming of age reads as a kind of parable about where the hubris of apparent success can lead. The bank was treading the same path as that of the country that sent the first man into space while simultaneously building a deeply insensate economic system. It was as if the surly, contemptuous cashiers of the Soviet grocery stores had simply been transplanted into branches of the bank. Newer parts of the banking chain underwent something of a Euro-style renovation, but the level of service remained abominable.

The grinding gears of this gigantic machine were operated by low-paid personnel who had no desire to consider either client convenience or the value of their free time. Zlatkis saw that the procedures the business operation functioned on were wretched and not fit for purpose. Kazmin estimated that investment in technical improvements at the bank had cost more than $1 billion, but this outlay had barely changed anything. Opening an account, clients automatically received a savings book, just as they had in 1841. Later, consultants would state that in its approach to IT the bank was still in the Jurassic period.

The bank itself, however, didn't think so. Kazmin's team was no more sensitive to outside criticism than the bronze statue of Nikolai Kristofari, the bank's first depositor, which stands at the entrance to the building on Vavilov Street. Viktor Orlovsky, who, before moving to Sberbank, had worked for the organisation as a consultant for IBM, was struck by the narrow-mindedness and haughtiness of his future employer: "People from the Department of Banking Technology who invited me to a consultation were barely interested in what I had to say. The majority of the meeting was spent demonstrating what we were doing wrong at IBM."

Sberbank felt invulnerable, nestled as it was in the bosom of the state. This incarnate security atoned for everything else — antediluvian technology, long queues, and rudeness. The company was too big and wealthy to make a drama from such minor shortcomings. Kazmin would admit that not everything ran smoothly at the bank, but as he presented it, these service issues were more the side effects of popularity. In an interview for *Kommersant* in 2007, Kazmin put forward the following argument: "There is a very high strain on our operational apparatus — seven times more than Eastern Europe, and around ten times that of Western Europe. They have 1000-3000 clients per service point, while we have 30,000-40,000".

Lord Victor Rothschild of the celebrated banking family saw the purpose of banks as "facilitating the movement of money from point A, where it is, to point B, where it is needed." Sberbank solved this problem in its own way. It was able to vacuum up citizens' savings thanks to the state guarantee and the ubiquitousness of its branches around the country. This money was then made available as loans, not for private individuals — these made up no more than a quarter of the bank's loan portfolio — but for

"It is also worth noting the high level of confidence and security from fraudsters offered by the Sberbank savings book in comparison to plastic cards."

Excerpt from the article "*Sberknizhka Sberbanka: v chem sekret populyarnosti?*", www.sberbank.ru.

businesses. In a system like this, retail banking was an optional extra. Essentially, the same applied to businesses, which would line up dutifully for loans on favourable terms, obtained by having connections at the bank. Applicants even came to Vavilov Street itself to ingratiate themselves with the right people.

The bank favoured major borrowers. These included Nafta Moskva owner Suleyman Kerimov, cement king Filaret Galchev, and Yelena Baturina, head of Inteco (and wife of the then mayor of Moscow). Such captains of industry were simultaneously major shareholders. Kerimov's stock alone, according to the Russian edition of Forbes, may have reached a hefty 6% by the end of 2005 (five years later the biggest private shareholder controlled all of 0.017% of the bank's shares, while among corporate entities this amount did not exceed 0.3%).

It was not clear that it was market conditions that were determining the granting of loans to big companies, who were inclined to buy up shares in the same bank and effectively dilute its capitalisation. However, as far back as 2002, Vadim Kleiner, Head of Research at British investment fund Hermitage Capital Management, who had joined Sberbank's supervisory board, publicly accused the bank of lending to major Russian corporations at undervalued rates. How did the bank react? Not by entering into a public spat; instead, it mounted an action in defence of its business reputation, winning the case with little difficulty.

This artificial inflation of capitalisation likely spelled the end for the management. Gref, as minister and member of the supervisory board at Sberbank, was not the only official to recognise the disastrous consequences of the endeavour (he said himself, with his usual frankness, that it had led to inevitable conflict with the bank's leadership). The game was so risky that even the Kremlin was beginning to feel uneasy.

Those in banking could only sigh — such squandering of colossal resources! If it had played its cards right, Sberbank could have been competing with the world's biggest banks. This competition could have been driven by a prudent lending policy, professional staff, modern technology and practical working environs — instead, it was based on its relationship with the state.

Zlatkis regarded Gref as one of the few people up to the task of civilising the bank. Gref didn't just understand that change was long overdue — he actively pursued it, heedless of doubters who considered reforms in such a bank doomed from the off. The will of a single, albeit influential man met a seemingly insurmountable wall of inertia at this enormous corporation. Gref's Western ideas held no sway with this intrinsically Eastern mindset.

What became of the dreams of those liberals seeking a European path to Russia's development? The further it progressed, the more the nation rejected the values of the emancipated West. Soviet nostalgia enjoyed a resurgence — the loyal state employee became the hero of the new era, and it was to them that most politicians began to pander. Young people ever more rarely saw themselves in business, preferring instead a steady income as an official or, even better, a manager at some large state company. Of all hypothetical freedoms, Russia evinced only one to any real degree — freedom of consumption. Private enterprise was on the decline. Willingness to work hard and inclination towards self-improvement

"In shareholders' meetings I would tally up amounts for producing reports, and I know the composition of our shareholders. We have don't have the major shareholders to propel shares."

Interview with Bella Zlatkis, *Ekho Moskvy* (12.07.2006).

and betterment of social status were characteristics comparatively few were disposed to exhibit. It was difficult to imagine a society less inclined to reform. Why should Sberbank be made of more pliant material than the country as a whole?

In regarding as foolish the government's decision over Kazmin's dismissal, Alla Aleshkina could consider herself the voice of a general consensus. Before the session of the supervisory board she did not lose her fighting spirit. Kazmin's wife wasted no time in restoring her husband's composure. There was no trace of the doubts planted in his conversation with Zlatkis; the president was sure of what position to take.

On 16th October 2007, Gref's candidature was approved by a majority. Three of eleven members of the supervisory board, Kazmin, Aleshkina and Zlatkis, voted against. "To this day it's dreadful to think back to how I felt at that point", admits Zlatkis four years on. The protest vote, however, was just the first act.

In the evening of the same day, it became known that seven of the board of directors, including Kazmin and Aleshkina, had sold up their shares. Kazmin explained this as his reluctance to take part in the extraordinary general meeting: "I'm leaving the bank, so it should be those who are staying that vote." A short time later, senior managers composed an announcement about the dismissal, recorded in the official account of events as being "at (Kazmin's) own request" and "due to taking up new employment".

Kazmin was still expected to appear at the shareholder's meeting at the end of November. Those present recall being moved by the rather dry valedictory address from the outgoing president. The hall remained on their feet, some close to tears. With Kazmin went an era of fairy-tale prosperity, during which the bank had made a fortune, shares had increased in value and dividends had grown. In the four months leading up to the meeting, the price of stock reached its historic peak, trading at 113.05 rubles per share. What now? Wasn't it ridiculous to think that this liberal dreamer from the government was capable of running the bank any better?

Gref, addressing the meeting after Kazmin, must have sensed the mood in the auditorium. He made no attempt to whitewash the situation he'd inherited: the bank had turned its back on its customers and hadn't adapted to their changing needs. This was a big problem, and one that required solving.

"We need to demonstrate that elephants can dance", announced Gref to a murmuring audience. "We need to create a versatile, market-reactive, saver-friendly and secure structure. Give me time, and you'll see what I'm capable of." The new president chose not to go into the specifics. He didn't tell shareholders that these dance lessons would herald the most unprecedented programme of change ever seen in Russian business, or that he and his team were about to install a radical new management system at the antiquated bank. There were too many disgruntled people in the hall, and any account of what awaited would have been tantamount to ridicule.

> "...for centuries our bank has lagged behind the world leaders of banking in a host of areas, primarily in technology."
>
> Letter from German Gref to colleagues (29.04.2010).

CHAPTER 2
THE MAIN STRATEGIST

GREF WAS REGARDED AS A MASTER OF PUBLIC performance, but he was not a born orator. Colleagues claim that he had once been pretty much tongue-tied. Old television footage records an incoherent address by the young minister in the corridors of the Bely Dom, the seat of the Russian government: a couple of statements about Land Code reforms garbled to journalists, encased in an armour of bureaucratese. However, Gref didn't need too much time to get over his handicap: with experience his speech became clear and authoritative. As a youth, he had learned to cope with adversity, developing an uncanny ability to pursue his aims with startling determination.

Gref was born in February 1964 in a small village in northern Kazakhstan: Panfilovo, founded by exiles from St Petersburg. His family had been forcibly evacuated to this distant backwater, miles from the regional centre, at the outset of the Second World War. At that time, virtually all ethnic Germans were subject to deportation. Viewed with suspicion due to their kinship with the aggressor, Soviet authorities kept them further from the front lines. "I've experienced more than a few awful things in my life," he said later, "starting from the day I was born. I could have grown up in a nice flat with lovely parquet flooring somewhere on Nevsky Prospekt. But fate decided otherwise."

German, the youngest in the family, grew up without a father. His mother ran the accounts department of the local rural council, while simultaneously taking on the running of the women's council and working at a local radio station. His grandmother was largely responsible for raising him. Neighbours recall the young Gref as a skinny, fastidious boy who was well turned-out even when sent to tend the cattle.

After finishing school, Gref wasted no time in taking his leave of his native backwater. After two years' national service in a special ops unit of the Interior Ministry, he continued his education at university, enrolling first at a *rabfak*, an institution designed to prepare workers for higher education. Of the reasonably respectable ones, the closest was Omsk State University (the Irtysh district of the Pavlodar *oblast*, where Panfilovo is situated, borders Omsk *oblast* to the north). Gref chose a subject that suited his meticulous nature — jurisprudence.

The future minister graduated with an honours degree. Later, Gref would confess that he had no time for straight-A students. He evidently did not want to be thought of as a calculating careerist, methodically setting out for himself a route to the top. Gref, by his own admission, wasn't particularly concerned with formal elements of study such as grades. "Somehow I got to my third year before realising I hadn't even managed a B", he recalled.

Gref didn't normally display much of a weakness for reminiscing about childhood and his younger days in public; accordingly, his biography during his ministerial years became riddled with myths. As with many Russian politicians, Gref had two biographies — the official one, and the off-the record version. According to the first, Gref rose up through the ranks quickly and without setbacks. The second affirms that there had been a few blips along the way. Immediately after finishing school, Gref purportedly went to Moscow and entered the Faculty of International Economic Relations at the Moscow State Institute of International Relations, but was in fact kicked out after two years of study.

However, in both versions of the biography, the picture emerges of a man not afraid to swim against the tide. Working as a legal consultant to the agricultural administration for the Irtysh district, as Gref did at the beginning of the 1980s, may have been a perfectly agreeable way for some people to while away the years in the limitless expanses of the Kazakh steppe, but the ambitious young man wanted more. He understood what he was capable of in life, provided he put in the effort — nothing was likely to fall into his lap.

Gref's strong-willed nature made him a very resilient character. In January 1999, the Volga saloon in which he was travelling to Kemerovo Airport hit a truck at high speed. Newspapers reported that he suffered a serious head injury and broke several vertebrae. He was admitted to intensive care and was not expected to return to full health. However, Gref was stubborn. Physical exercises, which many of us would regard as a form of self-inflicted torture, became a daily ritual for him. Every morning he would set off on a jog, no matter the weather or the location. Gref would not even allow himself a break while on business trips. As colleagues noted, it did not take long for him to make a full recovery.

Who knows how the hard-working young lawyer's life would have turned out had he not been in the right place at precisely the right time, as the political establishment that would go on to take absolute power in Russia began to emerge in Soviet Leningrad.

In 1990, Gref earned a place on a Masters course at Leningrad State University. His academic supervisor at that time was the head of the economic law department, Anatoly Sobchak (he eventually defended his dissertation, "Development of and perspectives for structural institutional reforms in the Russian economy", at the Russian Presidential Academy of National Economy and Public Administration in February 2011). Future Russian president Dmitri Medvedev, a fellow student at the time, helped poster for Sobchak in the lead-up to the elections. And while Sobchak was head of Leningrad's city council, he took on a KGB officer by the name of Vladimir Putin as an advisor. With Sobchak's election as the first democratically-chosen mayor of the northern capital, Putin became a key member of the administration, alongside Gref's future colleagues in the federal government, Alexei Kudrin and Dmitri Kozak.

Gref joined the St Petersburg district property management committee while still a Masters student. He rose rapidly through the service and quickly established himself at 'head office' — the City Property Management Committee. The head of the committee was Mikhail Manevich, who would become a major influence on Gref's reforming views over the three years they worked together. A friend and confederate of economic reformer Anatoly Chubais, Manevich was a strong advocate of wide-scale privatisation, recognising the state as legislator, judge and regulator, but not much of a property owner. Later, Manevich's colleagues would say that even though the marketplace was in its infancy in Russia at that time, in him St Petersburg already had an expert on market economics.

Gref's boss endeavoured to breathe life into the city property sector for which he was responsible. Manevich believed in the power of private property at a time when so much around was government-owned. He implemented a register of city buildings, establishing a basis for their market valuation, and, generally, strove to determine a civilised path of development for the market, control over which officials were forced to share with the criminal elements of the city. In the end, Malevich paid for this with his life. In 1997 he was shot by a Kalashnikov-wielding contract killer on his way to work (to date, neither those who ordered the killing nor those who carried it out have been brought to justice). Ten days after the tragedy, German Gref was presented as the new head of the committee.

Gref set about reforming the housing and utilities infrastructure of the city. In essence, he wanted to turn the remaining elements of the Soviet economy over to the market. St Petersburg was no easy ride — the city's splendid façades hid courtyards more in keeping with Hades than the Venice of the North. Almost every fifth resident of the northern capital lived in a communal flat. The dilapidation of the utility systems beggared belief, but no one was willing to do anything about it.

Gref didn't expect many plaudits for changes implemented in the housing office — popular reform is virtually an oxymoron, whether the heating works or not, but trying to instil a culture of competition among plumbers and electricians would prove to be an especially thankless task. The single-minded head of the property management committee became a scapegoat for everything. Communal flat dwellers took him for a meddler, while pensioners blamed him for the rise in utility costs.

Scandal even overshadowed the opening of a settlement for the descendants of Germans deported to Kazakhstan. Gref had decided, in an attempt to right a historical wrong, to offer them resettlement in Strelna, near St Petersburg. The construction of a few dozen cottages required no budgetary outlay, as the project had been funded by the German government. However, families of servicemen also had designs on the land, and the furore that erupted around an old public building that had been placed at the partial disposal of the re-settlers even attracted the attention of the public prosecutor's office.

Just before the August 1998 financial crisis, Gref moved to the capital. He was now working as a federal official in his capacity as Deputy Minister of State Property. A year later the 35-year-old Gref would get the chance to become no less than the country's top strategist.

As head of the government, Putin had proposed working out a strategy for Russia for the coming ten years to 2010. He already knew the man for the job. The development of the document was undertaken by a specially-commissioned fund, the Centre for Strategic Development, headed by Gref. According to its director, the grand project was sure to draw in hundreds, even thousands, of experts from various fields. It was the Gref strategy that first expounded the argument for doubling gross domestic product. Along with lowering poverty levels and reducing external debt as a means of supporting the state's creditworthiness, this was one of three goals later considered achieved (this was by no means the consensus view: the audit and consulting firm FBK assessed the task of doubling GDP at 59.2% complete). In all, there were around ten objectives set out in the strategy, only a third of which were realised in the allocated timeframe.

> "Those who have worked as civil servants for real and didn't just fill their boots know: it's ungodly work when you consider the effort, responsibility and thanklessness of it. You do menial work for peanuts, with no holidays, for months on end without ever hearing a thank-you, and all you get in return is more rubbish about you in the press."
>
> **Interview with German Gref, Forbes Kazakhstan (11.2011).**

Gref's induction into the Cabinet of Ministers was a done deal. Before Mikhail Kasyanov's government, there had been no such position as a Minister for Economic Development and Trade, and indeed no such department; it was specially created for German Gref. The long-standing and solid relationship forged back in St Petersburg between the new minister and the head of state was beginning to pay dividends — becoming first Prime Minister, then President, Putin continued to offer his patronage to Gref. When discussions with opponents became heated, the minister was known to warn: "I'll go to Putin — he'll back me up!" At the peak of his powers he was regarded as a shadow premier, and later, as likely head of the cabinet. Even before the start of his "golden years", Gref was being given high-value responsibilities such as production sharing agreements. He was then trusted with that holy of holies — the restructuring of the natural monopolies.

Even the *siloviki* had to reckon with Gref, as their counterpart from the economic bloc of the government demanded accountability in expenditure. The defence department was shocked by Gref's poking his nose into its affairs — it wasn't for him to decide what technology to use for the army, and at what price. At a government session in May 2004, Sergei Ivanov, defence minister at that time, reacted angrily to a draft bill on government procurement proposed by Gref's ministry. According to the bill's wording, any procurement taking place without tendering required a thorough explanation from the ordering party as to why alternatives had not been considered. Ivanov once asked prime-minister Mikhail Fradkov, later director of the Foreign Intelligence Service, whether he really needed to show that the sole manufacturer of nuclear submarines in Russia (the Severodvinsk-based Sevmash) had no competitors in the country. "Not me. Gref. You need to show Gref", he replied.

In government, Gref stuck doggedly to the liberal line. He didn't doubt the Russian economy's capacity to grow without government interference. Nonetheless, Gref's faith in democratic institutions had its limits. He was sympathetic towards what US philosopher Francis Fukuyama called 'soft authoritarianism'. Gref had always admired the successes of Lee Kuan Yew, father of the Singapore economic miracle. "At a transitional stage of societal development, one must choose between democracy and economic progress", Gref explained in the foreword to the Asian refomer's book, *The Singapore Story*. (Even as head of Sberbank, he still flies to Singapore every year for a business forum, attending working lunches with titles such as "The Singapore miracle: magic, or hard graft?") Russia, in which Western values are peculiarly intertwined with an Eastern heritage, didn't present itself as a hopeless conundrum to Gref. His lips would curl into a sardonic smile whenever conversation turned to finding a "third way" — after all, how much did we know about the first two?

The economy of Russia, meanwhile, was not developing the way the minister for economic development had hoped. Gref and Kudrin, once the most influential members of the cabinet, were now considered vestigial pillars of liberalism in the government. Shrinking the state sector, something Gref had championed from his St Petersburg days, had now been usurped by the triumph of state capitalism. By the end of the first decade of the 21st century, ministry officials such as deputy minister Andrei Klepach were beginning to admit publicly that the state controlled half the Russian economy, a figure many regarded as conservative. In international ratings of economic freedoms, Russia occupied an ever-sinking position. Rising oil prices drastically reduced interest in continuing recently instituted reforms. On the external economic front, things didn't look too rosy either. Gref was the main lobbyist for Russia's accession to the WTO, and once threatened a trade war with the US over its continual obstruction, but heightened emotions did nothing to accelerate negotiations on the issue (it took until 2011 to conclude talks).

"I suppose Gref began to feel growing frustration that he was becoming less and less able to get things done", argues Sergei Guriev, rector of the New Economic School and independent director at Sberbank. "Gref is the kind of person who at a fundamental level cannot bear ineffectiveness. He clearly feels that he needs to do things that he won't be ashamed of down the line. Things he can tell his children and grandchildren about. For him, that inner motivation is extremely important."

Gref the politician's star was on the wane. He later recalled that as far back as 2004 he had already decided to retrain as a manager. At one point, he became a record holder for the number of rumours forecasting his resignation. All of them crashed into Putin's unwavering support like waves against a cliff. In the end, though, the writing was on the wall. By the autumn of 2007, Gref was no longer part of the new government. He announced he was worn out and requested to be released to pursue a career in business. Years later, Gref admitted to journalists that part of the reason he couldn't remain in the service of the state was the "pittance" he earned: "I have young children, and I needed to earn enough to live on. Unless you have some kind of additional earnings, it's impossible to live on that money", he said in an interview with Forbes Kazakhstan.

No one expected Gref to end up in business. Unable to halt his arrival at Sberbank, Kazmin and Aleshkina got their own back by refusing to work under the new president. Gref was used to personnel shake-ups — as a former government minister, he had seen five prime ministers come and go. Nonetheless, it was a discouraging sign. "Everything was done here to try and make me fail as quickly as possible", he recalled. With the resignation of the senior management team, virtually the entire key leadership of Sberbank had abandoned him. Even the finance team left *en masse*, which for a bank was akin to a temporary heart stoppage. "Pretty stressful", admitted Gref.

The novice banker reinvented himself — the ex-official dispensed with the beard he'd cultivated for the eight years he'd headed up the ministry, and radiated with the energy of a man sure in his own vision. For him, this wasn't simply a new job — it was an escape from a dead end.

The ideas that had foundered at a national level perhaps had more potential within a company — Sberbank served as a perfect subject onto which to turn his energies. Like Russia itself, it gave the impression of a wealthy but poorly run organisation. Working on such a project promised the outgoing minister tangible results, something he'd often been missing in government. Those who observed Gref in his first few days at the new job were astounded by his zeal for this new undertaking.

The bank's new president spent his first morning inspecting the head office. Those present recall Gref

> "I feel much more comfortable as head of a bank. Politics, after all, is a tough business."
>
> Interview with German Gref on Vladimir Pozner's show *Pozner* (15.06.2009).

moving unhurriedly along the same corridors his predecessors had passed proudly through not long before. He glanced absent-mindedly round the empty offices of the former management team, before heading straight off to the cafeteria, heavy with the characteristic aroma of Soviet canteen food.

Gref was surprised and annoyed by the fustiness he encountered at every turn. He was keen to let people know that things were going to be different with him. One of Gref's first decisions was to order the creation of a gym for workers at head office, but even before that he demanded a complete overhaul of the cafeteria. Working round the clock, it was finished in 69 days. Upon completion of the renovation, employees of the bank had a modern facility to eat in, effectively doing away with the previously out-of-bounds dining hall for the bosses. Under Kazmin, it had fed the upper management, and access to other employees had been restricted. An Italian restaurant was opened in place of this old 'members-only club'. Prices there were appreciably higher than in the old canteen, but no one was restricted in its use. "We weren't going to go about fencing people off", said vice-president Stanislav Kuznetsov.

The diversity of Gref's new life in banking required fiendish attention to detail as he worked to familiarise himself with a dizzying array of procedures. An uninterrupted procession of documents would appear on his desk requiring his signature. At first, he spent time examining them properly. Gref was a workaholic in the most hopeless sense (one of his advisors, Roman Terentiev, assured me that his boss got by on four hours' sleep a night). It became commonplace for meetings and negotiations to run on past midnight.

CHAPTER 2 • THE MAIN STRATEGIST

Sberbank's IT director, Viktor Orlovsky, first met Gref at the end of 2007. He got to the meeting with his future boss at ten in the evening, breathless and ready to apologise for arriving ten minutes late. Even at Alpha Bank, where Orlovsky had once worked, he was rarely on time, despite their draconian fine system — $1,000 per minute late to directors' meetings. As he rushed to the meeting, Orlovsky couldn't possibly have expected to be waiting another five hours to be seen. An endless procession of important visitors were in front of him in the queue. There were so many illustrious faces among them that it was like flicking through a copy of the Russian edition of Forbes. He related all this to his wife in hushed tones the following morning, so as not to wake his newborn daughter. Gref himself had recently had a child, but by three in the morning, as Orlovsky at last entered his office, even the most probing psychologist wouldn't have discerned much in the way of a proud new parent in the new president — far more a man who'd just been handed a colossal stack of problems that no one had faced before.

CHAPTER 3
STRANGE THINGS

HUNDREDS OF THOUSANDS OF PEOPLE WAITED tensely for the new regime to show its cards. December's fragile hope that Gref wouldn't charge headlong into reform seemed a little more certain by February. Time went by, and, with the coming of spring, department heads and their staff began to scoff at their own misgivings — Gref wasn't as bad as he'd been made out to be. This sense of relief was short-lived. One after another, strange things began to happen at the bank.

On the morning of 1 July 2008, to their astonishment, employees opened their email to find a message from the president. The text began with the words: "Dear colleague, This is the first time I'm addressing you as an employee of Sberbank." Gref went on to request that the recipient sound out his or her neighbours' and friends' opinions on Sberbank as soon as they had the chance, and further, to check how well the floor had been cleaned in the customer area, and whether the flowers outside the entrance looked nice. The staff had expected to hear any number of things from the boss, but not a deep concern for the state of their working environment.

Gref continued: "There are 265,000 people working at Sberbank. One improvement made by each employee per day works out at 100 million improvements per year. 100 million!" This figure "has no meaning other than the fact that it's big and round and makes something of an impression on a credulous mind", wrote one user of an unofficial blog for bank clerks. But "a certain impression" was made by the very fact of the bank's supremo personally engaging with his staff (almost all Gref's letters were put together with help from his assistants, but the final editing was always left to him). Kazmin had no such habit of writing to the 'shop floor', unless one included circulars he'd signed. Gref, on the other hand, took it upon himself to do it on a monthly basis, even requesting responses be sent to his personal email.

In his first letter, the president informed staff that he was bringing in consultants — "the best in the world". But what for? "In order to look at the world in a different way, to move out of our comfort zone, and see how we compare with other banks." In former times, those offering professional services had for the most part hit a brick wall with Sberbank — no one there was interested in what they had to say. Boston Consulting Group had had more success than others, but only in the sense that the bank had paid the consultants for a draft of urgent reforms, only for it to end up mothballed anyway. In an interview to an in-house magazine, Aleshkina made no attempt to conceal her dissatisfaction with the competence of the experts advising Sberbank: "These distinguished consultants are used to working in countries where business is transparent and they don't need to double-check every figure. A few of them ended up offering their services, but came unstuck at the first task."

Gref, on the other hand, welcomed them with open arms. Sberbank attracted the *crème de la crème* of the consultancy world. Bain came in to fine tune the work of the bank's back office (i.e. the documentation and client operations services), and develop IT

> "Recently I received an email from a Nikolai B asking about who writes my monthly "Good morning, Sberbank!" messages and communiqués. My reply: despite my very busy schedule, I really do write each message every month myself."
>
> Letter from German Gref to employees (10.06.2009).

technologies. Fitch worked on the bank's revamped brand and branch design. Oliver Wyman helped develop a new risk analysis model for business loans. PricewaterhouseCoopers was trusted with developing a methodology for conducting geomarketing for the branch network. First off, however, Sberbank took on McKinsey.

This venerable American agency, founded in 1926, did more than anyone else to make consulting a standalone profession. Without McKinsey, consultants would still be drawn from the ranks of retired managers from disparate sectors. Thanks to McKinsey, those who'd never worked anywhere other than consultancy firms were now considered consultants regardless.

In the 1960s, expressions such as 'to McKinsey' and 'to be McKinseyed' entered daily use. This meant a complete reorganisation or remedial shake-up of a company. Subsequently, McKinsey developed their image as business chiropractors, carrying out large-scale research and helping clients launch ambitious start-ups. By the 2000s, the company name was generally coupled with the word "elite" in business literature.

In Russia, McKinsey had a hand in the development of Russian Standard Bank. Their business model, formulated by the consultants, was launched in 2003 when virtually no expert believed consumer lending to be possible in Russia. McKinsey's client had banked their success on opening up lending to the man on the street, and then presenting them with quite extortionate repayment rates. In 2006, Russian Standard admitted that, taking into account all commissions, this rate came in at a cool 55%. This greatly exceeded the level that in the US would be considered illegal 'loansharking'. Questionable from a moral standpoint, but from the point of view of McKinsey's client, it was sterling work from the consultants. Russian Standard Bank rode the wave of consumer lending adeptly, and led the market for a long time.

McKinsey was not noted for modesty when putting a price on its services. On average, a consultant would take home around half a million dollars a year — for this, the company would make its staff work for every last cent. Up to 80% of new recruits didn't last two years at McKinsey. Some lacked the qualifications, but most didn't have the stamina. During project commissioning, 15-hour days were routine. There was no let-up. The *up-or-out* policy, introduced in 1954, made no allowances for sitting around. Any mistake had to be learned from, and those who didn't progress were shown the door. In an atmosphere of continuous competition, the company became a meritocracy based on a 'survival of the fittest' principle.

As Christopher McKenna notes in his book *The World's Newest Profession*, an unforeseen consequence of the *up-or-out* system's implementation was the emergence of former employees loyal to the company. Many of these alumni went on to become successful managers in their own right at large corporations. A typical example of a McKinsey alumnus was Denis Bugrov, who at 33 was unexpectedly made the primary strategist at Russia's biggest bank.

Analysts were perplexed. In the spirit of Trudy Rubin's famous response to Vladimir Putin, banking journalists found themselves asking, in mock bemusement: "Who is Mr Bugrov?" Before Sberbank, Bugrov was perhaps known in the relatively tight circles of business consultants, or among graduates of the London School of Economics, French business school INSEAD and the School of International Economic Relations at MGIMO. By 2007, less than a year before he arrived at the bank, the McKinsey partner had been featured in the magazine *Finans* as one of the most successful young businesspeople in Russia. The following year, his success was confirmed: he accepted Gref's offer to become part of management at Sberbank.

The young man had the all the makings for a dazzling career. His father — deputy director and board member of the Interros group, Andrei Bugrov — had influence and numerous connections within business and diplomatic circles. By enrolling at MGIMO, Bugrov Junior was following in the footsteps of his father, who had obtained his degree from the same School of International Economic Relations in the year his son was born (spending time as assistant to the dean in later years). Among Andrei Bugrov's course-mates was future head of the Russian Ministry of Foreign Affairs, Sergei Lavrov. Bugrov sat on the board of directors for a considerable number of foreign and Russian companies, some of which were in public ownership. At RAO UES, one of Bugrov Sr's colleagues, sitting together on four separate boards beginning from 2004, was German Gref.

During a Q&A session with Siberian students on the subject of talent, motivation and careers, Denis Bugrov recalled that by his first year at university he was earning "considerably more than his bursary". The following year, the youngster went to continue his studies in London at roughly the same time as his father was working as advisor to the president of the EBRD in the British capital. Denis Bugrov ended up in the Moscow office of McKinsey in 1995, having

---

"As Mr Gref says, if we can show that new management techniques can be implemented with such results and such involvement and trust from the staff in such a large and complex organisation, with its rich traditions and foundations, then it'll be a landmark for Russia as a whole and for the business community in particular."

Interview with Denis Bugrov, *Sberezheniya* (23.06.2009).

had preliminary meetings in New York and London, where he'd met with McKinsey director Adair Turner, later chairman of the Financial Services Authority (and a baron to boot). Bugrov wasn't given a contract immediately, as there were no vacancies. However, he was eventually taken on as an analyst, and over 13 years rose to make partner. Besides Russia, Bugrov worked for McKinsey in the USA, Britain, Norway and in various countries in Eastern Europe.

Former McKinsey colleague Valentin Mikhov recalls Denis actively cooperating with Gref on projects for the ministry. Bugrov himself told me that he was already in touch with Sberbank's future president while he was still at the Centre for Strategic Development. Bugrov had been tasked with knocking out an effective presentation from a stack of paper bearing an extensive discourse titled "Strategies-2010", the type of task at which the consultants were were regarded as unrivalled masters. A few years later, shortly after Gref moved to Sberbank, Bugrov, who was involved in banking, called him, offering to meet. Later, Bugrov insisted that he wasn't after a job, but had approached Gref as a potential client (there had been no previous dealings between McKinsey and Kazmin and Aleshkina). In his own pointedly composed way, Bugrov outlined all the marvellous opportunities which would open up to a big bank that was willing to listen to an outsider's opinion. Gref had yet to assemble a team, and his instinct was to give the young man a chance to realise his vision for himself, so he simply hired him. "This guy has some brains", was advisor Alexei Sitnikov's pitch to Gref. Bella Zlatkis publicly described Denis, who bore more than a passing resemblance to actor Philip Seymour Hoffman, as a "sweet, clever and capable boy". Needless to say, for the upper echelons of such a venerable Russian bank, such boys were quite the novelty.

Gref's choice of senior managers was the next stage in the procession of peculiar occurrences. Gref's unflattering view of the workings of the bank was in stark contrast to its own senior managers' assessment. "The only thing you hear from them is 'we're the biggest, we're this, we're that.' It's much easier to deal with people coming in from the outside and see what's going on", Gref said. Nonetheless, existing staff didn't always understand who all these people were, and how they had earned the right to run such an enormous organisation. Many didn't carry the prerequisite gravitas. Group portraits of board members in 2007 and 2009, were they hung side by side, would bring into sharp focus the contrast between 'before' and 'after', with the Young Turks displacing a Brezhnev-esque politburo. The average age of Kazmin's team in the lead-up to his downfall was easily over 50. A good half of Gref's managers had not reached 40.

Their youth underlined how differently the new team looked at life and business. IT director Viktor Orlovsky was a similar age to Denis Bugrov. The youngest son of a distinguished gas worker, he had dreamt of becoming a journalist, but graduated from a communications institute in his native Tashkent. He had moved into banking at the age of 22. Orlovsky's knowledge and experience of information systems had interested the Uzbekistan office of the state-owned Dutch bank ABN AMRO. After a time he transferred to Amsterdam. Criss-crossed by canals, the streets of this magical city hung heavy with the scent of marijuana, with eager tourists scurrying to and fro in search of a good time. When Orlovsky left to return to Moscow, it was like coming down off the moon. At Alfa Bank he met with oligarch Mikhail Fridman, of whom the youngster had first heard only the day before. At the new company, things were more Darwinian. After the amiable Dutch, who never felt the need to raise their voices, Orlovsky felt like he'd been thrown to the dogs in the Alfa office. His call-up to Gref's team a few years later meant saying goodbye to his comfortable IBM office in Moscow, where he'd also attained a certain standing. But Orlovsky had ended up where he needed to be, later asserting that there was no better place to be for an IT manager than Sberbank during this period of change.

Many of those who chose to go with Gref were familiar with how things were done in the West — these cosmopolitan types with degrees from prestigious business schools knew their way round the City of London and the geometry of Canary Wharf like the back of their hands. It couldn't be said that this kind of experience was especially valued by the previous regime. Andrei Kazmin had spent a fair amount of time in Austria and Germany, particularly at Deutsche Bundesbank, Germany's central bank. But this had been at the start of the 1990s, and was no more relevant to modern banking than Kazmin's deputy, Alexandr Zakharov's time with the USSR Chamber of Commerce and Industry in Bulgaria. In this environment, only board member Alexander Brinza, who had time with Arthur Anderson under his belt (although the international auditing firm was at that time being rocked by accusations of complicity in falsifying the accounts of energy giant Enron) could consider himself the odd one out.

Now, bankers from Merrill Lynch and Morgan Stanley had taken the places of these distinguished veterans. For the first time, a foreigner appeared among Sberbank's senior management — international development was headed by Ilkka Salonen, a Finn (he left the team at the end of 2009). The arrival of another foreigner on the supervisory board, Indian American Rajat Kumar Gupta, was another unprecedented event in the bank's history.

The new independent director had spent 34 of his 62 years with McKinsey, and was one of its most successful CEOs. During his time in charge, from 1993 to 2006, McKinsey almost tripled in size. In that time, he had helped get the firm's Russian office up and running. After McKinsey, Gupta experienced a rocky business career. He acted as advisor to the General Secretary of the UN, and was independent director at both Goldman Sachs and Procter & Gamble. Two years later, his reputation was dealt a blow when he was suspected of insider trading, accusations that formed the basis for an investigation conducted by the US Securities and Exchange Commission. When Sberbank requested his services, however, there were no questions hanging over the influential businessman. The only murmuring was over the size of the remuneration offered to Gupta in exchange for his advice on strategy — €440,000, almost 20 times the amount awarded to other members of the board. The bank's generosity was peculiar, given that Gupta offered his recommendations remotely — as a rule, he wasn't able to take part in board meetings in person, since they were not prearranged.

The new faces at Sberbank weren't there for a holiday. Each one of them presented a very real threat to the bank's tranquil stasis. Seeing how backward the company was, this new cohort of senior executives struggled to work out what kind of future their

---

"Sberbank, like other similar organisations, has no scruples when it comes to the business reputation of who it works with. Moreover, the president has repeatedly defended Gupta to minority shareholders, who've called (Gupta's) appointment 'Gref's fancy'."

Alexei Bagaryakov, CPRF Parliamentary deputy, "Time to kill the appetite of Sberbank senior managers." *Pravda*. (08.06.2011).

predecessors had envisaged for the bank. But its staff gave no thought to giving in — who could be so crass as to bring down a system that had served millions of clients for so many years, from Kaliningrad to Chukotka?

CHAPTER 4
A PRISON FOR MONEY

MY WIFE AND I PAID OUR BILLS AT A VERY GENERIC branch of Sberbank, set into the bottom floor of an equally generic concrete high-rise, the bank nestling in at most 100 square metres. In his Cold War spy novel, *Tremor of Intent*, Anthony Burgess christened these grim Soviet spaces 'prisons for money'. Without doubt, our branch was one such 'prison'. Whenever I was in there, my only thought was to get my business done and get out as quickly as possible. But freedom never comes easily.

The number of people gathered to use the bank in our district at any one time was usually enough to block the entrance for anyone else coming in. Queuing was divided into two sections — outside and inside. After half an hour of standing in the cold, even the little warmth offered within those severe, prison-like walls coursed through my frozen body like vodka. Elbowing my way along the narrow corridor, I was well aware that I was facing a good 15 to 20 minutes to reach the front desks. Eventually I was able to see the clerks ensconced behind thick, bulletproof glass. Of the four windows, usually only two were manned, three if you were lucky. These women did not display the slightest interest in what was happening in front of them. Their faces expressed such profound indifference that I was willing to bet that, were a snowman to appear in front of them bearing a payment slip, they wouldn't so much as raise an eyebrow.

One of them I knew personally — my family shared a landing with her. Our neighbour was a lonely, middle-aged divorcee. We were never invited in, but we'd seen in her flat when she'd left the door ajar. Dirty and cluttered with junk, it resembled a second-hand shop. Perhaps she did not have the energy to tidy, or maybe her clerk's salary was to blame, too modest to allow her to buy new things. She'd return from work late, grey with tiredness. Night brought no relief — she admitted that she'd still see "those mugs" (Sberbank customers) in her sleep. "I'll see it out to the end of the year, then I'm getting the hell out of that pit", she'd vow to me when I bumped into her on the way to work. But a year would go by and she'd just carry on cursing and swearing, forgetting the promise she'd made to herself.

What would turn Sberbank's 'money prisons' into comfortable offices where employees weren't tormented by nightmares about their own customers? It seemed a miracle was required. But Gref did not believe in miracles. If the bank didn't change, it risked losing depositors, most likely for good. Of course, Sberbank was a part of the state — it wasn't going to disappear down the drain, as happens to private financial companies all the time, the whole world over. However, stability didn't guarantee devotion — the population of medium to large cities, where dozens of commercial banks operated, were in no way obliged to trust their savings to the least approachable of them. "The lessons of history must be heeded: empires that cannot adapt fall", Gref warned his staff.

The golden age of state savings banks — that is, banks whose main function was to attract domestic savings in the form of deposits — was in inexorable decline. The history of such banks, too long to

> "Sberbank is like Scylla and Charybdis — going there is horrible, but not going there is impossible. Users need the services of this monster of banking, whether they want to or not."
>
> Rosbalt (02.04.2011).

suddenly be curtailed, charted their rise and fall. At one point, they were regarded as a unique brand of philanthropy — such banks were a safe haven for the savings of people with low incomes, since they were invested in low-risk securities, designed to reap modest but regular returns. However, the rapid development of technology and new standards of service that appeared around the world in the last quarter of the twentieth century caught savings banks unaware. In Europe, the position of 'social' banking markedly weakened. Few people were content with a stable share of the market. Only the most dedicated, and ageing, client base remained. Many of the banks were simply pale versions of what they had been 30-40 years before.

This was the case in France, the birthplace (in 1796) of the first savings banks in history. In the Czech Republic and Poland, state savings banks were privatised, and shortly afterwards vanished from memory. The old-school institutions continued in Spain, Italy and Germany, but underwent a crisis in the industry across the board.

There had always been many unemployed and lower-income people needing financial aid and benefits among the 50 million clients of Sparkasse, one of Germany's oldest banks. However, as the population became increasingly self-reliant, the social security responsibilities entrusted to the bank by the state became less and less palatable. At the beginning of the 1990s, Sparkasse was haemorrhaging customers. Competition from Deutsche Bank and Dresdner Bank, who had made inroads into retail banking, forced savings banks to think seriously about their own efficiency. A movement began towards allowing the market to have its say. After Sparkasse lost its state guarantee in 2005, the bank let it be known that it had no intention of consistently running at a loss to appease politicians. Benefit claimants had their access to ATM cash withdrawals and overdraft facility limited. In addition, the bank more than doubled account charges on all accounts, including those of the less well-off, a move which caused outrage among civil rights activists and Socialists in the Bundestag.

In 2003, on returning from the World Congress of Savings Banks in Madrid, Andrei Kazmin was positive about how Sberbank was looking in the overall picture: "We've no reason to blush", he told the magazine *Kompaniya*, "we'll learn what there is to learn, but we can report with pride on the products we offer that they can't. 'They' being developed countries." Kazmin's bank genuinely held an advantage over its peers; unlike in Europe, Russian law did not restrict independent lending policy. Beneath the motherly gaze of the state, Sberbank was able to do well by obeying a business's natural thirst for profits. But was this business worth much on the open market? Examples from neighbours in the former USSR gave cause to question this.

On gaining independence, the republics of the Soviet Union did not give up on their financial monopolies — instead, they were passed on as a kind of inheritance. The Ukrainian Oshadbank, a remnant of the banking empire of the USSR, preserved its state-backed status, but was not permitted to lend to corporate clients. No one attempted to make a national champion out of it at the expense of the market. And the result: twenty years on, the bank eventually made it into the top ten largest banks in the country for assets and capital, even without the assistance of a large branch network and state guarantee on deposits.

In Armenia, the former republic-level branch of Sberbank was privatised, before being sold on to Russian bank VTB. Latvijas Krajbank also went into private ownership. At the time of its purchase in the mid-2000s, by London-based Russian banker Vladimir Antonov's Convers Group, this former Latvian branch of Sberbank had only a 3% share of the market. Earlier, Antonov had acquired Snoras, built on the foundations of the Lithuanian Sberbank of the USSR. He had begun his career as an investor in 1994, as a clerk in a Moscow branch of Sberbank. He was aware that its large branch network and highly trained staff would allow the bank to compete with the big foreign brands who, unlike in Russia, were forces to be reckoned with in the Baltic. Upon buying Snoras, Antonov's first act was to commend the bank's retail technology — as his second, he announced plans for its wholesale improvement with the assistance of McKinsey (these measures nonetheless proved inadequate in preventing the bank from later sliding into bankruptcy).

What did all this point to? That Sberbank couldn't allow itself to rest on its laurels. It cried out for a fresh outlook and a new strategy to chart the direction the bank would take.

Such momentous plans are rarely drawn up single-handedly. According to Gref, there were hundreds of people involved in putting together Sberbank's five-year strategy — "This isn't a paper we hired some consultants to knock up for us", he emphasised. It is fair to say, though, that there was one figure in the conductor's role, acting as something between an editor-in-chief and a draftsman. Ironically, this figure was Denis Bugrov, a man who had never run a business before, let alone one in banking, but who did have experience of strategic consulting.

"Why is the Bank Strategy such an ideal that we need to construct a whole set of priorities based on it? You promise incentives – many are so content with what they're getting that they'll not want to change anything."

Letter to German Gref from employee Dmitry Udoyev (11.02.2009).

Bugrov oversaw the drafting of Sberbank's strategic plan from his rented flat in London, noisily accompanied by his newborn child. He didn't find the work overly taxing. This plan of 'modernisation' was for Bugrov "not an especially complex text, analytically": it was simply an outline of the acute shortfall in standards which the bank needed to face up to, and the steps it had to take to overcome them.

Independent director Sergei Guriev recalled that, before receipt of the final document, the bank's management sent drafts round its regional offices. "We did it the right way", Bugrov assured — "we got on a plane and went round the whole country." The strategy was presented and 'discussed', critical feedback was received, and its most contentious provisions defended. According to Bugrov, much of the noise related to issues of secondary importance (e.g. how many client managers were required on the corporate side, and were they needed at all?). Retail, where the most significant changes were planned, barely concerned the old guard. It was the unloved child of Sberbank's business, far more devoted as it was to corporate entities. Whatever happened, no-one expected any unpleasant surprises from this poor relation, unlike the sections devoted to risk management, the back office, and, finally, organisational restructuring. In fact, what would eventually spell the end for the existing hierarchy was laid out in the text *sans* gory details. Nonetheless, a single passage about the "redefinition of functions and responsibilities between levels of management", and "a reassessment of norms of governance within the structure" looked sufficiently ominous to cause deadly panic. No doubt those who worked on the text purposely softened the edges to avoid tiresome and

> "The text of the Strategy, our Mission and values are accessible on the Bank's internal portal, and every employee should acquaint themselves with it. The main thing is not simply to acquaint oneself with it, but to conform to it daily."
>
> Letter from German Gref to employees (10.04.2009).

premature arguments. Life, as is often the case, turned out more radically than even the most bold plans had anticipated, but to lay all the cards on the table in 2008 would have meant entering into open conflict with the conservatism of regional management. Yes, the strategy shone a light on Gref's intentions, but only enough for it to be palatable to the upper echelons of the Sberbank empire. Later, this tactical victory was reinforced by the directive 'Sberbank strategy in its own words'. Lower and middle managers were charged with getting the document across to their subordinates in a more accessible form, so that, as Gref hoped, "every employee recognises his place and his role in our common endeavour".

The intentionally softened tone of the strategy didn't alter its direction. Bugrov and some 350 of his colleagues created a document that killed off any hopes of preserving Sberbank in its previous form. The dry, bureaucratic language didn't mask the evident enthusiasm of its authors. The few dozen pages of the strategy document were, in essence, dedicated to the same thing — how to change everything.

The Kazmin administration had had more than one strategy of its own. 'Development to 2012', a project that was launched a few months before Gref's arrival, had not embodied anything revolutionary. It was a comparatively short document that carefully laid out a path to "dizzy new heights". Had much changed with the new regime? Enough to be immediately obvious on first reading. Consider, for instance, this passage from Kazmin's strategy: "The bank's long-standing experience of a large-scale client base and branch network, guaranteeing universal access to services, creates ... a basis for strengthening our leading position." And here is the Gref alternative:

"The poor exploitation of two competitive advantages of the bank: the marketing network and client base, [is a serious shortcoming]." The old management saw the task to be "increasing productivity", but neglected to assess its current level — "singularly low", according to the new leadership. And so it went throughout the document.

The authors of the previous strategy outlined the future through the tinted glass of correct but utterly uncommitted phrases that had been sculpted like the contours of a Rolls Royce. The new document got to the nitty-gritty. Gref's strategy told employees honestly that in the course of reform, one in five would not make the cut and the rest would take on a heavier workload. According to the text, by 2014, the workforce would be reduced to 210,000 people, and productivity would increase by 50% (a yearly operational increase of 10%). For this, the bank intended to "free up resources for improving the quality of service and working more intensively with customers in selling banking products." The management announced that, henceforth, it was "totally oriented towards the client" and would throw all its efforts into turning Sberbank into a "service" company. Naturally, the transitional period could not be an excuse for glitches in the system: the implementation of any improvements was to be "phased", with "wide use of pilot projects and the organisation of parallel operations." The bank's revenues were not to be affected. Quite the opposite: everything was to be in place within five years.

Despite this, the main characteristic of the document was not its target figures. The strategy introduced projects that embodied the essence of the new Sberbank. Everything else depended on their success or failure: whether reforming ideas would be supported from below, or if they would simply become empty management slogans. Staff working structures had to be reorganised and personnel involved in the reform process with the assistance of a productive system that the management saw as "a new ideology of administration". Strangely enough, the main inspiration for this system turned out to be the Japanese car manufacturer Toyota.

CHAPTER 5
COMMON SENSE IS ALWAYS WRONG

IN THE 1930S, MANAGERS OF JAPANESE FACTORIES had every reason to regard their workers as third-rate. When it came to production output, they weren't a patch on the residents of Detroit or Cleveland. 25-year-old Taiichi Ohno, an employee of Toyoda Spinning and Weaving Company, was staggered to learn that it took a dozen of his countrymen to carry out the work of one American. "Does an American really make ten times the effort? Clearly, the Japanese are wasting their energies somewhere", decided the future vice president of Toyota and the founder of its production system.

The Americans had the edge in the art of managing people. At the end of the 19th century, mechanical engineer Frederick Winslow Taylor embarked on a series of experiments designed to demonstrate that workers could work many times more efficiently, provided they were equipped with detailed instructions on what to do and how to do it.

In Taylor's understanding, the nature of the heavy labour to which factory workers were accustomed had virtually nothing to do with high productivity. The average worker was not only indolent, but was too stupid to be capable of improving productivity without guidance. A scientific approach was required. Taylor's guinea pigs were workers in a steel plant that worked pig iron. Armed with a stopwatch, Taylor carried out a time and motion study of the quickest workers. A veritable Dr Frankenstein, he assembled his ideal workman from different parts to determine the quickest and most precise processes. Bringing them together, Taylor produced a model for improving efficiency, which in turn became a standard for the whole workforce. The plant saw a fourfold increase in its productivity, while the workers received a sizeable salary increase. Taylor himself got his due, garnering world renown for his achievements. His epitaph describes him as the "father of scientific management".

Henry Ford continued Taylor's legacy. The legendary industrialist took the idea of labour efficiency to its famous conclusion with the development of the conveyor belt. Fordian mass production was regarded as a model anywhere industrialised technology emerged. Taiichi Ohno was among those who marvelled at Ford's genius. In 1943, he moved into the automobile business of his lifelong employers, the Toyoda family. At that time, Toyota Motors was primarily involved in supplying trucks to the Imperial Army. This wasn't to last — in the middle of August 1945, Toyota's biggest customer ran into terminal difficulties, namely defeat in the Second World War. Japanese militarism was buried in the rubble of Hiroshima and Nagasaki. The Japanese automotive industry had other plans, however, and endeavoured to rise from the ashes. Toyota didn't follow the example of other Japanese manufacturers, who immediately after the war decided to assemble foreign cars, especially American, on license. The company was sceptical of scientific management in the Western mould, when everyone else around was desperate to implement it. Toyota didn't share these values of mass production. By that time, economies of scale weren't simply a tradition — they were an axiom. Their foundation was strengthened by popular notions such as the Maxcy-Silberston curve, which firmly linked growth of output to falling production costs. However, for Toyota, merely trying to cut costs seemed inadequate, and in an expanding market, simply reckless.

"Common sense is always wrong", Taiichi Ohno loved to say. He believed that producing a wider range in smaller batches would one day spell the end for large-scale production. The company could allow itself a similar model only by radically revising its approach to managing overheads. Ohno declared war on waste. In Japanese, Toyota's main adversary was known as *muda*. In the widest sense, *muda* was something that created no value for the user and swallowed up the resources of the company. By analysing the nature of this wastage, Ohno got closer to answering the question that had troubled him in his younger days: what was causing the low productivity of the Japanese? There was clearly wastage somewhere.

Ohno identified seven different types of *muda*. Waste was caused by defects, waiting, surplus inventory, superfluous tasks and transportation of materials, over-processing and over-production. This was all systematically eliminated. Ohno's most ingenious innovation was the 'just-in-time' concept, in which a production manager synchronised the working of the full production chain, from delivery of materials and components to the assembly of the cars. No less important was the fact that the factory floor would no longer be governed by a production programme based on sales of the preceding batch, but on current demand. The company instead took orders from the market and set about completing them without delay. Ohno adapted a supermarket procurement system for his factories. In any self-respecting shop, sales of goods at the till serve as a signal to the warehouse to replenish these items on the shelves. At Toyota, the function of the warehouse was carried out by production. With the help of a new system of communication — *kanban* order cards — Taiichi Ohno was able to ensure that workers got the necessary components from each other at first asking. Components travelled in an uninterrupted stream from one stage of production to the next. Toyota endeavoured to make sure that not so much as a screw was delayed along the route to final assembly, and, ultimately, the customer.

Ohno said that he'd sought out "a means of making production work for the company in the way a human body works for its occupant". He radically simplified the passage of components through the factory floor, turned workers into multitasking machine operators (one operator for multiple functions), and taught them to work in rhythm with the daily flow of orders. All these changes had far-reaching consequences.

The 1973 oil crisis hit Japan hard, dependent as it was on hydrocarbon imports. Economic growth, which had lasted for 20 years, suddenly ground to a halt. Many companies went into the red, and a wave of bankruptcies swept the country. As for Toyota, it registered slightly lower profits than expected. In the 1980s, Toyota hadn't just caught up with America for productivity, but was cutting into its market. The big Detroit three, Ford, General Motors and DaimlerChrysler, could no longer count on the loyalty of their customers. Jingoistic patriotic appeals to the hearts of Americans with slogans like "Be

American — buy American!" largely had no effect. In 2007, Fortune magazine wrote, "25 years ago, it was just one of a herd of Asian interlopers selling fuel-efficient econoboxes, and Detroit snickered at the notion that Americans would ever want to buy many of them. As everyone now knows, that crystal ball was cloudy: Toyota's Camry has been the bestselling car in the US since 2002, and the Lexus LS 430 has been the leading luxury-car brand for seven straight years."

The Americans could only watch and learn. Hordes of managers and business consultants poured into Japan from the US. Everyone wanted to know how the Japanese had managed to cut the warehouse out of the production cycle, synchronise its work with a multitude of independent contractors (the number of Toyota's suppliers was approaching 160) and, most remarkably, build this entire system on the shoulders of the average worker, whom Taylor had written off as a weak-willed bag of muscle in his trials. With the 1986 publication of an English-language version of consultant Masaaki Imai's book, the Western world became acquainted with another important Japanese word — *kaizen*. This system of continuous improvement explained why Toyota workers had willingly submitted to the inexorable logic of its production machine. The firm had cultivated a culture of self-improvement both at work and at home. In doing so, it had bred a self-motivated workforce, intolerant of defective products, breakdowns and mistakes.

In the US, the Toyota system got a new name — *lean production*, since to the American mindset, Toyota's production carried as little excess weight as the average Japanese teenager. Under this label, the system went on to take over the world, granting

"As far as I understand, the main philosophy behind lean is people. Whether customer, worker, boss or his subordinates, we are all people independent of our social standing. And we all want heath, happiness, love and understanding."

Letter to German Gref from Veronika Zheltysheva (Perm) (07.02.2009).

everyone the chance to get on board with this new business philosophy.

Japanese wisdom reached Russia quite a bit later. The industries in the country that had managed to survive under the rubble of the planned economy couldn't spare the outlay. Running a business the Japanese way did not enter the heads of either the old Soviet-era managers or the new breed of Russian capitalists. Cherry blossom didn't bloom in Siberia. Nonetheless, Japanese ideas trickled into Russia alongside Western investment. In 2003 Gilbert Holmes, director of a Caterpillar assembly plant not far from St Petersburg, delivered a lecture on the utility of Japanese methods for retraining local workers. By that time, the Japanese system had been embraced by engineering plants the world over, including in Indonesia, where Holmes had previously worked. Russian factories were among the last to catch up. Pneumatic tool manufacturer Instrum-Rend, whose factory was based in the town of Pavlovo in Nizhny Novgorod Oblast, was taken on by parent company Ingersoll. Taiichi Ohno believed that the production system he had created was not suitable for stable and profitable companies. Success in its implementation would come about as a result of deep malaise within the company, which would force it to act. "This is the one advantage of those who are closest to death", he concluded. Instrum-Rend was one such hopeless case. Skilful adjustment of technical processes, which was met with approval even by Mercedes's ferocious auditors, had been preceded by a fight for survival. "When I am asked what made us do this, I respond truthfully: fear", factory director Vadim Sorokin told me. "We were acutely aware that if we didn't fix the problems [with the standard of production], we'd lose our jobs and wouldn't be able to feed our families."

By the end of the 1990s, both in the West and in Russia, lean manufacturing had already become far more than simply a metaphorical stool under the noose. The system had become a free pass to a world of low overheads, where no one would suspect how close you were to bankruptcy. American lean consultants were invited to GAZ, owned by successful billionaire Oleg Deripaska. Lean was put into operation in the holdings of another Russian oligarch, Severstal head Alexei Mordashev. Eight years ago, general director of Sollers (still Severstal-Auto at that point) Vadim Shvetsov was already talking about implementing elements of lean manufacturing and waxed lyrical about the work of the Dutch consultants whose experienced eyes were identifying *muda* on the factory floors of the Zavolzhsky Motor Works.

These examples of the emerging management system all shared a common grounding in industrial manufacturing. This made sense — the Toyota system was born and raised on the factory floor, among workstations and manual labourers. But remember what Taiichi Ohno said about common sense — there was something quintessentially irrational about the fact that the first large-scale implementation of lean in Russia was undertaken not by car manufacturers, but by the institution that was providing the loans to buy them.

CHAPTER 6
I KNEW NOTHING ABOUT LEAN

IT IS HARD TO IMAGINE RUSSIAN CAR FACTORY managers and workers following the way of Toyota. But a Russian banker acquainted with the self-same manufacturing system, if only in theory, was no less of an oddity.

"TPS — ever come across it?", Gref inquired of Vladimir Cherkashin, head of the Urals Sberbank. Cherkashin had no recollection of any such abbreviation. The 56-year-old banking veteran, with his gentle voice and manners, both unusually delicate for his status, was the first of the regional managers to speak with Gref face to face. It was a meeting between a staunch reformer and a loyal representative of the old system.

Like Gref, Cherkashin was born and spent his childhood in Kazakhstan, in the city of Semipalantinsk (later renamed Semey), near one of the Soviet Union's largest nuclear test sites. As a youth he moved to Sverdlovsk (now Yekaterinburg), where he devoted himself to an academic career. Cherkashin was a promising student at the Ural Polytechnic Institute (UPI). Russia's first president, Boris Yeltsin, at that time the first secretary of the Sverdlovsk Communist Party regional committee, had personally pinned the "For outstanding study" badge to Cherkashin's lapel. He later went on to be a lecturer in his alma mater's

CHAPTER 6 • I KNEW NOTHING ABOUT LEAN

department of economics and engineering plant organisation.

As capitalism took hold in the former USSR, Cherkashin decided he could make a living through offering financial services. He started off with a small financial investment firm, before going on to head the board of SKB Bank, in local terms the favoured son of Mikhail Khodorkovsky's Menatep Bank, where Alla Aleshkina had worked before moving to Sberbank. Cherkashin felt indebted to Kazmin and his wife — in 2001 they had entrusted him, an 'unknown', to manage the Urals Sberbank, whose area of operation encompassed hundreds of branches in the Sverdlovsk, Chelyabinsk and Kurgan Oblasts, as well as the Republic of Bashkortostan — an area roughly the size of Spain. Then, a few years later, the Moscow administration, with which Cherkashin had enjoyed a good working relationship, disintegrated.

In January 2008, Cherkashin was called to the capital — Gref wanted to see him. Having no idea what awaited him, Cherkashin decided not to make any special preparations for the meeting. He didn't really understand why Gref regarded Sberbank as this cloddish elephant, and could only guess what lay behind this urgent summons. Was it a prelude to his sacking?

Kazmin's spirit still lingered in his old office (Cherkashin had already visited it a couple of times in his time at the bank). Gref sensed Cherkashin's nostalgia, but didn't jump to any conclusions. Over the course of the two hours, Gref spoke at length about himself, and listened to his guest talk about his own life, cordially inquiring after the health of his mother. Then the president smoothly segued onto the subject of the bank's new management model:

"TPS is the Toyota Production System, the Japanese car company's own famed system." For Gref, this was more than just a passing fad — he had been a fan of the idea for a number of years. He became even more impressed by the system when he learned of the effect it had had at Japan Post Bank, one of the biggest savings institutions in the world, where it had been just as successful as in manufacturing.

"I made up my mind that one day I'd definitely try lean in Russia", Gref told me. "I remember trying to sell the idea to anyone who'd listen." Even before his arrival at Sberbank, Gref had been proselytising to colleagues in government and the ministry. Alongside his penchant for garish orange ties, his peculiarly specific interest in creating environments for facilitating ultra-productive labour and workers' personal development was one of the minister's eccentricities. At that time, post-Soviet Russians learning from Toyota seemed about as natural as them taking lessons in *ikebana*.

Many of these Japanese ideas were seen as insultingly simple. For the economists and sophisticated finance types I spoke to, they offered all the intellectual stimulation of a nail file. "Handy thing for a bank clerk", hissed one of them condescendingly about *kaizen* (small daily steps to self-improvement from every employee). It was like some molecular gastronomist sneering at scrambled eggs.

Cherkashin's response was different. When Gref posed him the question about Toyota, he seemed enthused. "Just-in-time, *kanban*, could encourage innovation among the personnel", Cherkashin suggested. He'd first come across the Japanese way of doing things in the library of the Bruno Leuschner School of Economy in East Berlin, where he spent

CHAPTER 6 • I KNEW NOTHING ABOUT LEAN

ten months in 1985-86. In his time working at UPI, he filled his lectures with the things he'd learned about Toyota working practices, but since then, this knowledge had been filed away in the furthest corner of his mind. He would never have guessed that, so many years on, it would suddenly become so useful. Gref was glad to have discovered someone who felt the same way. Cherkashin would later go to on assist in the development of the bank's five-year strategy.

For Gref, it was much simpler to present the essence of his plan to clued-up people like Cherkashin, but were there many such types in Kazmin's Sberbank? Were there any at all? Gref couldn't allow himself to get bogged down in discussions with those couldn't get their heads round it. There was no room for wavering among senior figures at the bank if the undertaking, which Gref compared to performing open-heart surgery on a galloping horse, was to be a success. At the first meetings of regional leadership, he declared his intentions and issued his orders: "You know, it's like in the army", explained Cherkashin, "You attack when you're ordered to. If you won't, then get off the front line."

In Russia, changes need to be carried through quickly. "Otherwise, they generally fail or grind to a halt", asserted Sergei Witte, another Russian finance minister — one of a different era, but with no less experience of carrying out large-scale reform. Gref hit the ground running: Sberbank's revival would begin with lean. And why this method, specifically? Gref wanted tangible examples of working processes to hand, something he could show off to sceptical colleagues and shareholders: see, it works. At the same time, the system guaranteed changing the value system of employees more rapidly than anything else, and making the staff more inclined to subsequent changes. Words like 'Toyota', 'lean' and *kaizen* became part of the strategy: "*Kai* — change, *zen* — good", explained a footnote. Reform at Sberbank would begin with the toughest challenge — changing the company's mentality.

If it wants to, a small company can comparatively quickly modify the thinking of its staff, at least outwardly, through the 'high conductivity' of its decisions. Inevitably, with a bank of Sberbank's magnitude, the task was an epic one. According to McKinsey, the bank needed to carry out between 1,000-2,000 lean adjustments to fully realise the system's potential. The main challenge was assembling the teams to carry out the changes on the ground, as they had to understand banking procedure, be able to identify problems and offer solutions to them. It took at least six months to train every member of these teams, and McKinsey estimated they should consist of 0.5-1% of the total workforce, roughly 2,000 people at Sberbank. To roll out the system as quickly as possible, McKinsey were invited to open so-called 'lean laboratories', in which selected employees would undergo a course of training before setting out to put their new-found knowledge to work. In this way, it was possible to assemble a critical mass of lean experts within the specified time-scale.

The first lean labs appeared in Moscow, Nizhny Novgorod and Barnaul. Normal branches were used to host them. Televisions were installed to keep those queuing entertained, and coffee machines were introduced, as the scent was said to have a calming effect. Diligent staff were placed in the branch reception, and the clerks smiled and worked more swiftly than usual. This was only what was visible to the customer — behind the scenes, a war was being waged on waste. It lurked everywhere — in procedure, in workers' movements, even in fittings (for example, the cumbersome corded telephones on the clerks' desks). *Muda* was the recurring theme of the daily (morning and evening) and obligatory "five-minute brainstorms". In its own way, the bank was replicating the quality control circles and productivity groups devised by Tokyo University professor Kaoru Ishikawa at the end of the 1960s. A curious feature of the laboratories was the way staff were permitted to circumvent the usual rules and regulations at the bank for the benefit of customers and to make cost savings. For example, it became clear that, of the 20 obligatory procedures required for replacing savings books, 15 were utterly superfluous.

There was no question of simply relying on complicated and costly IT solutions. From the outset, the bank had consciously been trying to rebuild itself without cutting corners. It started from the bottom up, trying to improve efficiency by making money already pumped into the company work better for the bank. Staff began to see their jobs in a new light — obsession with order and diligence became a habit, which in turn became a compulsion. "It's really infectious. Workers are going home and implementing lean strategies there", Anastasia Ponomarenko, who took charge of one of Sberbank's lean labs soon after their launch, told journalists. It was a becoming a passion. No-one in management had expected this: the phlegmatic Denis Bugrov had talked about the bank's metamorphosis in such a dispassionate tone that it seemed he'd expected it all along. "People have a fire in their eyes; their faces are bright and smiling. People seem 'infected' with their own successes", said

Gref of his impressions of the lean lab in the Donskoi district of the capital.

Nadezhda Polezhaeva, senior clerk in one of Sberbank's offices in Moscow's southern outskirts, described the atmosphere in her team to me differently. "Many were slurring from tiredness and were at their wits' end. People were permanently stressed because they didn't know how, when and what they were supposed to be doing. Some of my colleagues were panicking that they'd be left without a job." The study "Lean production and disability", which collected data of workers' health issues in Dutch firms, suggested that a third of these were directly linked to psychological conditions. Perhaps the sensitive Dutch were overplaying it, but lean was no picnic. "People's muscles had atrophied, their expressions blank, shoulders hunched — basically, they were on the edge of nervous collapse", was the picture one former employee of a Sberbank branch in Vladimir Oblast painted of the end of average day.

Gref rushed events along regardless. At the start of autumn 2008, he'd hurriedly assured staff that the system would be in place in every main branch by the end of the year, and for every member of staff by the middle of the next. He wasn't going to hang around. Managers at the Moscow headquarters snapped at the heels of their subordinates, demanding action. But this tempo couldn't be sustained. The project proved more difficult to roll out than expected. What was going on?

Let's imagine for a second what kind of people the bank selected to fire the first shots of this lean revolution. The average 'revolutionary' woke up to the alarm tone of the latest iPhone. He slipped into an expensive suit, enjoyed a leisurely coffeehouse breakfast, before getting behind the wheel of the BMW he'd bought with his last bonus. At the same time, the average clerk was waking up to a spoonful of instant coffee and hastily doing her make-up, hoping she could grab a little extra sleep on the Metro carriage before it reached her stop. They were from different worlds, but their paths crossed at Sberbank. Although it had all the makings of a melodrama, this was where the movie parallels ended — no realisation of shared interests, no overcoming of clashing worldviews. From the 'revolutionary's' point of view, the workers hadn't a clue about efficiency — they didn't really know what work was. The workers, on the other hand, liked the routine and quietly despised the sneering big-shots who wanted to destroy it.

In Russia, productivity was a sore subject for many banks, not just the biggest ones. A study into the Russian retail sector conducted by McKinsey in 2009 demonstrated how far it lagged behind even its Eastern European neighbours, let alone Western markets (although in terms of numbers working in banking, at a little over 400,000 Russia was comparable to the US, the Netherlands, Switzerland, Spain and Poland combined). For example, to carry out a payment transaction, a Russian clerk had at least twice as much to do as his or her Polish colleague (21 steps to the Pole's nine). In the States clerks worked seven times more efficiently than in Russia, while in Switzerland the gap was nine-fold. For a while, Sberbank had even managed to fall below the low standards McKinsey had calculated as average for the Russian banking sector. There was scope to question McKinsey's workings — if they'd used the simplest and most common means of assessing performance, looking at banks' cost-to-income ratio, Russian banks would have seemed perfectly healthy. To calculate this ratio, the bank's operating expenses are divided by its gross income, plus any depreciation of fixed assets. This relationship between "what has been reaped" (the final return) with "what has been sown" (what has been invested as expenditure) broadly reflects a bank's performance within a particular country. The world leaders in this are the Spanish, whose average score among that country's top ten banks is 45%. Russian banks come in behind British and Swedish banks in fourth place with a ratio of around 50% (i.e. for every rouble spent, they got two back in revenue). The most disappointing results are those of the Germans, at 73%.

This is hard to believe. Over the past few decades, Spanish banks have deservedly been among the elite, but the land of the siesta is hardly renowned for productivity, and it wouldn't occur to anyone who has ever been in a German bank to compare them to the Russians. Sure enough, the results of McKinsey's studies demonstrate a very different assessment, as they use their own Retail Banking Productivity Index. It is worked out using a rather complicated formula based on basic banking procedures. Here, the Spanish exhibit a third of the productivity of the US (which is taken as the base for calculating the index), while the Russians demonstrate only a tenth. Against the Americans, even Russian builders compare better than their bankers for productivity.

Gref's mission was made all the more difficult by the fact that, unlike the manual labour of those builders, banking required mental exertion. What bank clerks produced was measured not so much in the number of transactions completed or the queues they'd busted, but in the more nebulous concept of quality of service. It would be odd to judge the performance of a university professor on the number of students that attended his lectures, or a doctor on the number of admissions (though sadly, this is often the case in Russia). The questions that matter are those concerning quality, not quantity: do the doctors have the expertise? What state of health are the patients in?

Peter Ferdinand Drucker considered increasing the productivity of intellectual labour the most important task facing 21st-century managers — this giant of management theory was still hard at work on the problem well into his eighties. Born in Vienna in 1909, he emigrated to London in the 1930s, where he worked as a banker. Over the next seven decades, which were spent in the United States, he devoted himself to the study of management in its various incarnations. Drucker knew that the world was nowhere near developing effective management methods for those who worked more with their heads than with their hands — even developed countries were far from a solution. By the turn of the millennium, assessing the intellectual output of workers had become a major area of research. In 1900, studies into the productivity of physical labour were at the same initial stage, with tentative attempts to attach numerical parameters to a workforce's labour. Responsibility for productivity, this "source of all economic values", had to lie ultimately with independently motivated workers themselves. According to Drucker, they should become the managers of themselves.

But the average Russian, like those who worked in Russia's state bank, did not live in Drucker's ideal world. This reliance on management, the fear of making decisions and taking responsibility lay deeper than any desire to organise oneself. The initial stage of Sberbank's reform was more than an attempt to

"I urge you all: be in charge of yourselves. Be your own bosses."

Letter from German Gref to employees (27.05.2010).

try out Japanese know-how on the clerks; it was the age-old conflict played out between management and a staff who wanted only to be left in peace. Were any of the architects of this new lean-bank fit to be agents of change? Someone who knew the old system from within had to be the best person for the job.

Gref suggested Maxim Poletaev, the up and coming young head of the Baikal Sberbank, as the man to develop the project. The youngest among the heads of the regional branches was already something of a legend. In Irkutsk, where he'd arrived from Yaroslavl in 2002 as the new head of the board, he'd been considered one of Aleshkina's men. Other versions of the career progression of the 31-year-old manager, such as his success in previous roles, did not give such cause for optimism, but regardless, Poletaev was quick to find common ground with his subordinates. In the Baikal bank, he is still remembered as the man who got air conditioners fitted for both customers and staff. His incognito Saturday visits to branches have not been forgotten either. Spooked by their young boss's eccentricities, the tellers circulated his photograph, but the modest hat and Chinese puffer jacket in which he disguised himself allowed him to conduct his covert surveillance undetected.

Poletaev wasn't seeking to catch anyone out: according to those he worked with, he was merely trying to form an unbiased view of how service was delivered — why employees worked they way they did, and how.

Perhaps it was all in the poor working conditions. Many tellers spent their entire day cooped up in their cramped and gloomy branches. Poletaev spared no effort in upgrading his branch network. The bank needed new and spacious offices, and worked continuously on improvements, but nothing would change overnight. In some places, workers didn't even have an adequate toilet. Allegedly, a furious Poletaev nearly fired the entire maintenance department when he learned that facilities had been laid outside in the yard. This was no joke in a city like Irkutsk, where temperatures dropped below -40 °C.

Poletaev's Hawthorne experiment proved a success. By methodically introducing more agreeable ways of working with staff, he was able develop a support system for the production pacesetters. In the large but sparsely populated regions labelled "economically depressed" (Irkutsk Oblast, Buryatia, Zabaikalski Krai), Poletaev's bank not only served customers, but actively sold financial products, primarily loans. Local branches managed to shift tens of millions of dollars of American Express traveller's cheques, a product whose popularity was not so prevalent even in Moscow. During the financial crisis of 2008, the Baikal branches showed the best profit performance per employee in the Sberbank network.

Poletaev is not one for questioning management decisions (in response to a number of my questions, he told me to contact Gref's office). It was no surprise then that when Sberbank's president phoned him in 2008 to suggest leaving Irkutsk to implement the new management system around the country, Poletaev dutifully obliged.

What did Poletaev know about lean? "When I was offered the job, I didn't know a thing about lean, a fact I told Mr Gref straight out", he recalled, "But the boss said I'd be up to speed soon. I should be ready to for the job in a few weeks."

The first discussions on how to reform the bank did not fill Poletaev with much enthusiasm. He and his colleagues had their doubts: "We were really against it, we just didn't understand what Gref expected of us."

From the outset, Gref wanted him to get a view of the bank and its condition as a whole. Poletaev spent a week at a South African lean academy, where he set about getting to grips with the basics. His trip to Cape Town gave him a better grasp of the overall aim of the lean philosophy, an understanding supplemented by reading *Lean Thinking*, published in translation in Russia in 2004, on Gref's instructions. While still minister, he'd enthusiastically foisted hundreds of copies of the book onto government staff and business figures. The authors, American James P. Womack and Englishman Daniel Jones, were long-time fans of Japanese thinking and strived with characteristic persuasiveness to bring them to the West. "Forget everything you used to know about value", these pioneers of a new order proclaimed. Poletaev found the book hard going, but, in the end, useful.

In it, Womack and Jones bowed before Taiichi Ohno's creation and outlined the inferiority of traditional mass production. The book was written in the '90s, by which time the Toyota system had already celebrated its 30th birthday, but companies still clung to their old beliefs about business. Womack and Jones lamented how little regard was paid to the customer. As they never tired of repeating, anything that did not create value for the client was *muda, muda, muda*. From this perspective, the majority of management decisions, production procedures and routine activities carried out by employees seemed superfluous or detrimental. Millions of tonnes, miles, hours, dollars and pounds were rendered *muda* every day. However, the book's grim diagnosis was supplemented by a precise course of treatment. How was a company knocked into shape? To what extent were the Herculean efforts necessary to start thinking and acting on lean principles worth it? Reading *Lean Thinking*, the world seemed all messed up, but with a reassuring potential for change.

James P. Womack was so convinced of the fundamental power of the doctrine that at the end of the '90s, he set about demonstrating it by example. Together with colleague Guy Parsons, he took control of the struggling bicycle producer Merlin Metalworks in Cambridge, Massachusetts. Womack and his partner did everything that was required: they conducted a thorough inventory of the shop floor, reduced the amount of stored materials to a day's supply, sold off excess equipment and dispensed with warehousing finished products. After this crash diet, the company was set for financial recovery. Sadly, the bank's credit officer didn't see it this way, and flatly refused any further provision of vital credit to Merlin Metalworks. Visiting the plant, he did not appreciate the efforts against the forces of *muda*, but did notice an empty warehouse and zero accounts receivable. "You just don't have the assets", he had concluded. With failure on the cards, Womack and his companion sold the company to industry specialist American Bicycle Group.

After Cape Town, Poletaev went with other senior Sberbank managers to Toyota to see with their own eyes how its legendary system operated. Toyota had accumulated a rich arsenal of equipment, the precision and efficiency of which many regarded as fantastical. The head of one automobile component plant in the Urals who had also visited Toyota compared it to Disneyland for factory floor bosses and production directors. I remember him talking a great deal about the "just-in-time" delivery system, and lamenting that, in Russia, such a vision was still the preserve of only the most hopeless idealists.

The Russian bankers' impression of Toyota was also twofold. Indeed, they had gone to Japan for the experience, and no-one had disappointed their expectations in that regard. But after observing how the cars were put together, no matter how masterfully it had been organised, the managers were still left shrugging their shoulders: what could it offer the post-Soviet financial services market? Gref bemoaned the lack of practical examples to follow. "For service companies, these programmes are not applicable", he had said. "Here's where the difficulty lies: there's no-one we can borrow a well-worked-out system from."

Was it only factories that had anything to learn from Toyota? Of course not. In the world of finance, lean had long taken hold, Alexander Idrisov of Strategy Partners (a Russian consultancy firm acquired by Sberbank in the summer of 2010) assured me. By McKinsey's count, a number of major financial firms had implemented lean methods, including Barclays Bank. Perhaps unsurprisingly, it was the experience of Latin America, and not Japan, that had sparked Western bankers' interest in the system. In 2003, local partners of McKinsey unearthed evidence of particularly successful lean implementation by Chilean banks. Chileans are not blessed with serious resources — they work in a market where poor customers offer less revenue and are more expensive for the bank to service as a result. But by utilising lean techniques, as well as changing the format of branches and centralising back office work, they were able to drastically reduce their cost to income ratio. Consultants spoke of a potential 40% reduction in expenditure. The rapid success of measures which limited the need for major investment was enough to jolt the banking world out of its indifference. Sberbank's interest in what was happening in Chile is unclear — obviously, recent examples of successes at big European and American banks seemed more sound and culturally more relevant. Credit Swiss and Citigroup, for instance, had adopted a concept that had been devised by consultants seeking to reduce wastage in car plants.

Gref himself had been impressed by the way lean had helped centralise the back office functions of UniCredit. The Italian group's experience was perhaps more suited to Sberbank than any other. Alessandro Profumo, the ex-head of UniCredit, became advisor to Gref, before joining Sberbank's supervisory board. Another member of Sberbank's board was Ilkka Salonen, who had long been head of International Moscow Bank (which later took the name of its parent, UniCredit). Vice-president Bella Zlatkis (whose daughter had worked for UniCredit in Moscow) often had often pointed out the similarities between Sberbank and the Italian company.

However, something prevented Sberbank managers pointing to any one of these examples and proclaiming, "That's it!". Short trips to Western banks such as the Scandinavian Nordea group were instructive, but their usefulness was not worth overestimating. "We were shown wonderful things that we really wanted to implement at home", Poletaev said, "but Sberbank wasn't at a stage where we could get this done. Compared to the post-industrial methods of Nordea, we were living in the Stone Age."

In all, Poletaev devoted eight months to rolling out lean, but this was enough for him to have his baby,

> "Did anyone, let alone Gref himself, give any thought to how much the names of these corrective programmes grate on people from the former Soviet Union? SPS, 5S – it's like fingers down a blackboard."
>
> Forum post on 'Comments on working at Sberbank', www.banki.ru (11.10.2011).

his colleagues had joked. He took the pilot offices that, though scattered around the country, were still very much removed from real life, and made something of a bank-wide system from them. This wasn't the worst result for a man who couldn't remotely have imagined beforehand what he was undertaking. Gref had made up his mind earlier that if Poletaev didn't let him down on lean, then he'd be sent to Sberbank's Moscow business, which was to stand at the vanguard of reform. Gref would have no cause to regret his decision, but more on that later.

By that time, it had been decided that on its Japanese (quasi-American) foundations, Sberbank would build its own management platform. The company was to hold on to the sacred principles of *kaizen*, but would deploy on a broad front in the battle for efficiency, assimilating anything that would help the cause. Sberbank's production system went into action under the abbreviation SPS (ПСС), replacing the foreign-sounding lean. Despite the efforts of management to introduce it, this process was in general independent and organic, judging by the internet forums. One employee suggested, instead of the rather dry SPS, calling the system "sustainable bank stewardship" — the suggestion was politely rebuffed.

The system took root, becoming something of a dogma in the eyes of its most staunch supporters. "SPS is our everything", Yulia Aizup, head of the eponymous department, told me quite firmly. She was convinced that the production system offered the bank a "competitive advantage", which would make it possible to "raise the quality of service to world-class". It's very important, she added, that those who had set the bar in Moscow didn't have their head in the clouds, otherwise all that wonderful theory would bear no resemblance to the daily realities of a clerk in Siberia, something Aizup had once been herself.

In the West, "management by walking around" had been a popular ritual since the upper echelons of major corporations realised that they had lost touch with the realities of the shop floor. Introduced in the 1980s by Tom Peters and Robert Waterman in their business bestseller, *In Search of Excellence*, management by walking around forced management honchos to descend from their ivory towers. While serving as consultants for McKinsey, the authors had run into a Hewlett Packard design-engineer in a shop — he was manning the till. The US electronics manufacturer did not allow its hotshots to remain cloistered for long. At McDonald's it had grown into a tradition — every 15th April, on the company's birthday, managers would leave their offices to spend a few hours at the coalface. IKEA's management also do the odd shift on the shop floor, while a similar spectacle is witnessed whenever the chain opens a new branch, as senior managers help customers with their packing. In his memoirs, the general director of the Swedish furniture giant's Russian operations, Lennart Dahlgren, recalls an incident during the opening of the Kazan hypermarket in spring 2004 — a woman and her child were queuing at a till where the company's founder, Ingvar Kamprad himself, was labouring away. Pointing to the silver-haired billionaire, the mother warned her son: "If you don't stick in at school, you'll end up like that old man over there, packing people's shopping for them in your old age."

While you are unlikely to come across one of Sberbank's board members behind the glass of your local branch, Aizup assures me that all of the bank's senior management, from Gref down, are obliged

"The bosses have been going on Gemba walks, but by no means all of them, and it's not really caught on."

Forum post on 'Comments on working at Sberbank', www.banki.ru (05.02.2012).

to go on Gemba Walks, or to put it another way, to spend time "in the field". Deputy chairman Stanislav Kuznetsov, who among other things oversees the bank's cash couriers, once spent a day in one of their armoured cars ferrying money around the Moscow branches. To prove it, he showed me photographs of himself bedecked in uniform and body armour, surrounded by a squad of heavies.

"Go and see for yourself" is one of Toyota's fundamental principles; Taiichi Ohno assigned it huge importance. He would have his subordinates draw a circle on the factory floor and, without leaving it, spend the entire day observing what took place. Sberbank managers initially considered Gemba a poor joke on the part of their bosses, but in the end reluctantly acquiesced and went out to the branches. What they saw was no surprise — endless queues.

CHAPTER 7
THE 5S DEEP CLEAN

IT IS DIFFICULT TO EXAGGERATE WHEN IT COMES TO the queues at Sberbank. 440,000 man hours lost, suggested a study commissioned by the bank in 2006. Every year, customers spent enough time queuing at the bank to lead the equivalent of 80 average Russian lifetimes. The typical wait for a customer to pay a utility bill was 42 minutes.

During Kazmin's reign, queues were considered a congenital defect, and customers suffered them in the same way they suffered the Russian winter: there was nothing anyone could do about either. There were too many things that customers needed to do at Sberbank; the close timing for payments of salaries, benefits, pensions, and utility bills led to branches being besieged like medieval fortresses. Every second day there was a rush to make or claim some payment or another. In busy areas, there was little respite at all. "If you scrawl 'Sberbank' on a wall in chalk, about 30 pensioners will start queuing", ran one joke that appeared on the bank's in-house blog. The Russian Union of Pensioners did not see the funny side, and the wag was quickly fired.

Valentin Morozov was one of those took a fresh, analytical approach to the issue of queuing at the bank. With a little bit of calculation, this insurmountable problem could begin to be resolved. Before he arrived at Sberbank, Morozov had weighed in at almost 19 stone. The head of SPS implementation (and the

"If we're going to lie, even about little things, we're never going achieve our aims."

BBC interview with German Gref (19.08.2001).

latest of the McKinsey graduates) lost more than three stone battling the bulge. The war declared on excess weight dragged in other managers at the bank, including members of the board. The extra pounds hit their pockets too, since shedding them was a major component of the key performance indicators that decided the size of their yearly bonus. The bankers, lounging in the leather-upholstered seats of business class, would compare distances for the following morning's jog. The calorie-heavy treats that passed by on the trolley remained largely untouched. The bank was run by a fitness fanatic who had never struggled with his weight. It was the done thing to follow his lead. On meeting a group of portly bosses from the bank's logistical services, men happy to splash out on ludicrous modular buildings complete with apertures for cash machines and air conditioning units suspended triumphantly from the ceiling, he had exploded. "Lose the weight, or we lose you: 20 percent, no less", he had told one sweating, pot-bellied unfortunate. "Lean" production meant exactly that.

The branches, straining under the weight of the queues, were to shape up too. "We started with the basics", recalls Morozov. "We got rid of the simultaneous staff lunch break. We made one general queue from the multiple queues to various windows." Dynamic scheduling of lunch breaks allowed for more even handling of the customer flow, not to mention an end to the rather awkward spectacle of the bank closing its doors on its own customers for its staff to eat. Before, customers had needed to go to different windows for different services, and hence wait in different queues. With tellers able to carry out more functions, a single queue system began to cut waiting times.

Next, the average working day of a typical bank clerk was broken down into segments and reassembled minus the superfluous details. "We estimated that processing utilities payments alone took up just under a quarter of our staff's total working time. In Sberbank terms, shaving ten seconds off each such procedure would free up hundreds, if not thousands of people," said Valentin Mikhov, head of the bank's Department of Strategy and Development.

In some regions, they were able to reduce the procedure from two or more minutes to 45 seconds. The key improvement was the acceleration of data entry, 30% quicker for those who could touch type, and a general streamlining of the process. It reached a point that clerks stopped using staplers, allowing customers to staple their own receipts and cheques (a practice later discontinued due to the customers' dawdling). However, in some places, only technology offered a solution. According to Vladimir Tarankov, head of the Department for Development of Commission Transactions, clerks worked faster when they were provided with devices that simultaneously counted notes and verified their authenticity. The effect was amplified as soon as branches were equipped with a system that identified customers by scanning their passports, cutting a four-minute transaction down to two.

Takt time, another nod to Japanese assiduity, was another addition to the branches' arsenal. Takt time could be thought of as the rhythm of demand-driven production, a worker's taskflow. A better analogy would be that of a couple of dancing. Imagine there's no music, and you can hear only your heels tapping. If you, as the leading partner, could not hear the beat, then you would not get anywhere. You have to have the melody and rhythm in your head — provided you can hear these, the dance progresses in measured, harmonious steps. Sberbank's raging torrent of customers created more of a racket. It was hard to step to the same beat with each of them. As a means of relieving the queue situation, it offered no quick fixes. Only cutting service times would protect the delicate choreography.

The arithmetically-derived standard was up to three minutes at peak times and no more than five at normal periods. In the branches, the bank began to install electronic queuing systems, which automatically calculated average service times. IT bosses broke their backs to meet Sberbank's technical demands. No-one else in the market was capable of supplying the capacity it required. 500 electronic queuing systems were produced in Russia per year, and there were only 30 teams trained to set them up. However, the bank needed 4,000 units, and aimed to have them purchased and set up over five months using 100 teams consisting mostly of hastily trained recruits. The heroic effort undertaken by the teams to complete the biggest order of their lives ran into no less epic setbacks. In many places the electronic display did not work. But despite it all, the retail division did not allow the pace to let up. In places where electronic queues were either absent or not working, calculations were conducted manually. "A 'monitor' sat behind the girls with a clipboard and stopwatch, timing each transaction", observed a former employee of the Siberian Sberbank. Quarterly statistics influenced the size of staff bonuses. The bar seemed to many to be set too high; staff grumbled that the figures set out from on high defied the laws of physics. The time allocated to serve customers while at the same time answering all their queries was far too short. The complaints were dismissed — there was enough time, provided it was used wisely.

Have you ever seen a spaghetti diagram? Unsurprisingly, we are talking about something confusing and illogical. I once saw such a diagram drawn in coloured markers on a large sheet of chart paper. It was hanging in the director's office of a factory in the Volga region and consisted of two parts: the first showed the actual course taken by parts on the way to final assembly, and was a complex figure full of crisscrosses and circles; the second path was many times shorter. Weeks of continuous observation of activity on the factory floor had gone into the charting its epic passage. Every conveyance of parts and materials and every worker's movement was marked on the map. Afterwards, the results were analysed. In this way, miles of unnecessary movement were identified. It was all direct losses, *muda*. Sberbank's compact little offices offered little room for thinking about efficiency. But when there's a will... A little bit of ergonomic placement of furniture and equipment, such as moving the photocopier closer to desks, cut down on the extra miles and lost hours.

At the Japanese car manufacturers, they were prepared to consider initiatives that would save no more than seconds. Gref said the same things, but in different units: "It's possible to use every square centimetre efficiently and effectively." The president reckoned that the task was best tackled using the Japanese 5S methodology. The five words, which all begin with S in their transliterated Japanese original, stand for 'sort', 'straighten', 'shine', 'standardise' and 'sustain'. Not everyone at Sberbank was enraptured with the new system. At first, many female staff

"Three years ago I would never have thought that Sberbank would become a more or less normal internet bank, that it'd be smiling young workers serving you instead of sour-faced old battleaxes, that it'd have electronic queues. Sberbank has finally emerged from the Dark Ages."

Forum post on Sberbank, www.habrahabr.ru (11.02.2011).

> "Of 17 windows, only one was open, at which a large and 'lively' queue had formed (the automated system wasn't working)."
>
> Blog of National Reserve Bank owner Alexander Lebedev. (13.01.2012)

members regarded it as no more useful than instructions for washing floors or scrubbing potatoes. They were indignant, accusing management of patronising them. It is easy to see where the women were coming from. 5S counselled workplace tidiness, something any house-proud person would regard as their own prerogative. Moreover, the system was so basic that grown adults felt like they were back at school. It was like being scolded by the teacher for blotting your jotter, and Sberbank already had enough such pedagogues. What did 5S preach in the office environment? Correct filing of documents and stationery storage. It also taught employee discipline, upon which a clean, organised working environment could be established. In such a setting, clerks would not have to keep disappearing to get the right type of paper while the queue bayed. This was the theory, at least. The reality?

"Instead of rewriting the stupid instructions and cutting down on paperwork, SPS disciples are 'reshaping space and time' by moving tables around and doing time-motion studies", read one of the dreadfully libellous comments on the banking forums. Ways of cutting waiting times for customers had turned into formalist self-indulgence and nonsense in the eyes of the staff. The forums reveal how staff were taught the best way of arranging the bins to optimise the passage of rubbish. During a review of workstations, spare pens on the tables were declared surplus. I was told about one clerk who almost lost her monthly bonus for accidentally leaving make-up on her desk. At another location, the boss used a ruler to measure how evenly boots were arranged on the shoe rack, and demanded photographs of children be removed from desks since they did not directly

CHAPTER 7 • THE 5S DEEP CLEAN

relate to work. "Today 5S got applied — everything got scrubbed with bleach", said one worker at a Moscow Sberbank about her branch's preparations for a planned inspection. At head office, underlings shook their heads at the overzealousness: "And they call this SPS! They have no idea how much that idea has been distorted."

In Western companies, this phase had to some extent passed. Administrative pressure had led to sabotage, but as soon as people had been convinced of the objective benefits of the system, they came round to it. Today, even such a simple set of maxims as 5S has a dedicated fan-base worldwide. Back in the '70s, when interest in Japanese management styles was in its infancy, the system had made a big impression on the Americans. In an interview with The New York Times, a director of the old school shared his impressions of 5S: "At first I didn't see anything special in it. Then it hit me: they were all creating profit. No-one was messing around looking for parts, waiting to be told what to do."

The war on long queues at Sberbank began by putting the paper clips in the right place — but a tidy desk did not make for radical change. The bank went further, moving on to the organisational structure of the branch network itself. With pen and paper, retail director Alexei Chernikov (who became deputy head of the Central Russia division of the bank) explained to me how Sberbank would look were it a standard European retail operator. Looking on, it seemed he was drawing up a battle plan. "Here's our district. Suppose we have the flagship office, around which we have a group of supporting standard offices. These in turn have their own network of smaller, specialised sales offices, plus separate cash machines and terminals."

> "There's a set of instructions for 5S. There's also the wisdom, 'keep things clean and tidy'. What more is there to say? Yet these instructions run to 40 pages."
>
> Forum post on *'Comments on working at Sberbank'*.
> www.banki.ru
> (23.01.2012)

The meaning was clear. Multi-format offices — general and specialised, of different sizes and capacity — were much better suited to dealing with a varied client base. It allowed someone coming in for a loan to avoid being stuck queuing behind old ladies there to pick up their pensions. The other extreme — disproportionately large branches serving only a couple of blocks — was dealt with in a similar way. Tiny self-service offices no bigger than a bedsit could be opened in their stead. Natalya Gribkova, director for relations with branch offices, was convinced that in five years the system would completely change the way customers thought about Sberbank as a savings bank. At the same time, the long queues would become a thing of the past. Gref promised that average queuing times would be halved, no more than a quarter of an hour at peak times, though 85% of customers in city branches would not wait more than ten minutes on average. Since then, this figure has been rounded up to 90%.

But what would follow? Would the end of queuing also mark the beginning of the end for SPS? Gref was concerned — the ardour seemed to be cooling. For two years, the system had encompassed more than 100,000 members of staff in 8,700 branches (the majority, if rural branches are not counted, since 60% of these had only one member of staff). The economic effect, a third of which was down to lowering outlays and the rest in additional sales, amounted to a cool $1 billion. What more could Sberbank want for? When Bugrov, the system's curator, proudly reported its success to Gref, the response was not wholly congratulatory: the staff's enthusiasm for it was on the wane and SPS needed a second wind, of which there was no sign. "I didn't know at that point what

"At the moment, there's a perception that SPS has been landed on everyone from on high, that it's only the bank itself that needs it and that there are no pros whatsoever for ordinary members of staff. But that is fundamentally not the case!"

Moi Sberbank interview with Julia Aizup, Director of the Department of SPS Realisation and Banking Processes (03.06.2011).

more I had to do", said Bugrov. "I found that out later." Having dreamt of unleashing a system of unceasing improvement at the bank, Bugrov was now sure he was still far from achieving his goal. The production system showed no more indication of its capacity for autonomous development. Moreover, something of a rivalry between lean and IT as to which was more effective had developed at the bank. Automation had been the easy option, but the lean camp flatly rejected any technical upgrades without tangible results. If processes are not perfected and people work wastefully, then microchips will be no good, assured lean's defenders. They were also quick to point out the performance improvements lean offered for such little outlay.

Gref himself continued to regard SPS as the cornerstone around which everything else was built, the successes technology offered included. "Computers and robots do not increase productivity. People increase productivity", he countered, an objection he was willing to retract only when artificial intelligence had been perfected. "It's not likely in the next hundred years, I think, but we'll see", he joked.

According to Bugrov's assessment, of the overall 40% growth in productivity, 25-30% of this was purely down to lean, but only after its initial introduction. Later, this halved to 15%. This downward trend pointed to the fact that lean now needed to be adapted to the challenges of the 21st century. 46% of Russian city dwellers surveyed by market research firm Romir said they used online banking services regularly. Many had begun paying their utility bills on the Internet. There had been a rise in the popularity of payment terminals, which, according to research conducted by TNS, were periodically used by four out of five Russians. The goalposts had shifted, and front office staff seemed increasingly like rowers paddling frantically to make a speedboat go faster. People being organised and efficient was all well and good, but what if new technology could replace clerks, even the quick ones, with the click of a button? Pragmatism dictated that to reach global standards of service, SPS would have to forfeit its leading role. Doubts emanated from the company's nerve centre — the board. Alexander Torbakhov, who had joined the bank in autumn 2010 as deputy chairman of retail banking, could not hide his scepticism. He had far more faith in an IT revolution than he did in *kaizen*. "We really didn't see eye to eye on this. My problem with SPS is that I can't fully convert him to it", admitted Bugrov.

Nonetheless, converts among the bank's rank and file were particularly enthusiastic. They saw the system as more than just the manifestation of managerial despotism, but as an opportunity to express themselves. The bank experienced a wave of innovation. For a Russian company, an incredible number of people wanted in on the act. It had not been the mechanism of continuous improvement Bugrov had hoped it would be, but regardless, ideas for improvement abounded. Many, many ideas.

CHAPTER 8
THE CREATIVE CLASS

OVER A NUMBER OF YEARS, A CHASM HAD OPENED between the bank's upper echelons and its rank and file. It seemed peculiar to imagine the creative force of the bank being in the hands of anyone but management. Change, whatever it affected, was the prerogative of a narrow elite at the top of the corporation. No one looked to its thousands of employees for any ideas. "The talent of such a huge number of people was not being put to use. That kind of wastefulness really surprised me at first", recalled Valentin Morozov.

Tatyana Svidunovich, a former manager at the state-bankrupted oil company Yukos, was charged with dealing with the problem. At Sberbank she ran the Banking Processes Office, where she faced the daunting task of presenting the sensible ideas of its employees to the bank's decision-making centre.

The project was called "The Market of Ideas", and there were some doubts regarding its usefulness to a bank famous for its elaborate bureaucracy. Through sheer force of will, management was imposing a production system that was beginning to face increasingly fierce resistance. Why would people intent on dragging the bank back to the old days suddenly rush to bombard it with their own ideas for improvement? Wasn't this logic a little flawed? "The Market of Ideas became my pet project", Svidunovich told me. She was sure of its worth: instead of having them imposed from above, the staff would drive reforms themselves.

Svidunovich could look to IBM for inspiration. Ten years ago, the company brought together 300,000 employees to exchange experience and provide professional advice and assistance to each other. The aim was also to guard the enormous transnational corporation against signs of disconnection that seemed to be creeping in, as more and more employees worked from home or at their clients' premises instead of IBM offices. This was the first in a series of so-called 'jams', large-scale online brainstorming sessions from which IBM harvested ideas. Many more were to follow. In 2006, the best ideas to emerge from the 150,000 participating employees formed the basis for ten new IBM businesses, the company pledging $100 million for their development. "The best organisations measure how well they are doing using only two parameters — the ratio of ideas offered to the overall number of employees, and the percentage of these that are implemented", said Gref.

It was tempting simply to copy the experience of IBM, but this turned out to be a false start. "We wanted groundbreaking ideas, but none emerged", recalls Svidunovich. However, this call for the staff to "expand their minds" did not fall on entirely deaf ears. It garnered a response few anticipated — not a couple, or even a few hundred, but tens of thousands of suggestions for improvement flooded head office. The bank's rank and file now felt part of a great undertaking, in which any useful solutions they were able to offer could potentially have a major impact throughout the country. The principle was familiar from Soviet times, when even the lowliest milkmaid was encouraged to suggest anything that might

More than 55% of Sberbank branches are located in small towns and villages.

Data from 2010 Sberbank annual report.

increase yields. The national economy of the Soviet Union, even in the final years of its existence, remained keen to harvest the ideas of its most resourceful innovators, even if by this stage implementing them was a little like rearranging the deck chairs on the Titanic. The unharnessed creative energies of the Soviet people at least had an outlet.

Sberbank made every effort to make it easy for staff to offer their ideas. A quick online registration, and employees immediately became part of the company's social network. Those who didn't want to use their real names could join anonymously. Every suggestion submitted was examined by experts to assess any economic benefit it could offer: if there was none to speak of, it received a polite thank you; if there was moderate potential, payment of between 25,000 and 50,000 roubles was offered depending on where it was to be implemented. For the ideas that offered the most potential for savings, the bank promised the person who had come up with it 10% of any savings made up to maximum of 1 million roubles.

The project quickly grew into a large-scale campaign. Many wanted to share ideas that, if successful, could make them some money. In the space of two years, around half the workforce signed up to the "Market". A third of all savings ideas were related to Internet banking. Other popular subjects included loan products and retail procedures. Svidunovich was particularly fond of ideas that simplified documentation processing, such as doing away with superfluous duplication when making up account cards for each client. Thanks to the canny observations of its employees, the bank was able to shed most of the annual cost of notarising copies of its appendix-heavy charter when they discovered that, legally, one document instead of the usual nine sufficed. Net annual savings amounted to 32 million roubles.

Even the cash-in-transit guards were not exempt. At the end of every day, each squad was required to sign back in to indicate their return, a procedure that took up 20 minutes of the senior guard's time. The other men would go outside for an extended cigarette break in the meantime. One guard worked out how many such squads were killing time in this way — there were approximately 14,000 cash guards serving 130,000 locations at Sberbank. And what exactly was the point of this long-standing ritual? "We looked into it, which turned out to be a good idea: there was no legislation that required it. The bank itself had at some time or another introduced it as a rule, but it wasn't clear why it still needed to be followed", said Svidunovich. Eventually it was decided that the registration procedure was only to be carried out in the event of a traffic incident or attack. The rest of the time, the squads would not be required to file any reports at all. The person who drew attention to this received 225,000 roubles.

In the first two years of its operation, the Market of Ideas earned or saved the bank 8 billion roubles. The staff began to warm to the idea, overwhelming their employers with more and more new suggestions, although at most one in ten were ever explored. The deluge required sorting, assessment, and expert analysis. At head office, the bank seriously considered creating a separate department for innovation.

In 21st century Russia, innovation was the buzzword of the day. State propaganda assured the populace that the President and his government were committed to making innovation on a par with mineral wealth as a driving force for the nation's economic growth. Gref's own economic development ministry developed a national innovation strategy to 2020. Even the Federal Notarial Chamber got its own Centre for Innovation, while the Federal Forestry Agency announced it was about to open two such centres itself. Sberbank, too, was not immune to bandying the word around: "Encouraging innovation is one of the key objectives of the Sberbank Production System", wrote Gref in one of his monthly communiqués. "Those who innovate, our 'creative class', will be the ones who go on to greater things here." On one floor of the Sberbank Novosibirsk head office, management even decided to create a 'gallery of innovation'. The corridors began to resemble something from Star Trek, with wall-mounted monitors and dynamic lighting set into the floor, illuminating the space with the aid of colour filters and mirrors. 'Conceptual' would likely be an interior designer's assessment.

However, such collective thinking had its limits. Sberbank continued to resemble a peasant urging his horses onwards against the din of combine harvesters. The inventiveness and innovation of its staff allowed the bank to progress rapidly, but weren't enough on their own for it to catch up with the rest of the market. More drastic steps were required.

> "On Saturdays, colleagues should go on a Gemba walk, visit different offices, and have a period of self-study."
>
> **Letter from Gref to employees (30.09.09).**

CHAPTER 9
NO MORE DOING THE SLIPS!

'DOING THE SLIPS' IS RUSSIAN ACCOUNTANCY JARGON for signing off on small pieces of financial documentation such as payslips or receipts. For Sberbank senior vice president Olga Kanovich, this awkward expression encompassed a fortnight of training at one of Moscow's savings bank branches, undertaken when she was a student at the Plekhanov Academy of Economics at the end of the 1980s. Kanovich would have to put little ticks on printouts of data produced by the old computers, before matching it to information in the handwritten records. The young student detested this tedious and unglamorous task. At that stage, working for Sberbank was the last thing she wanted from life.

Fate got the better of Kanovich. In 2008, she was one of the first to join Gref's team. Luring a board member of VTB 24 bank was no mean feat for the president. At first, Kanovich didn't even want to meet; when Gref's headhunters eventually managed to arrange a meeting, it proved fruitless. Kanovich couldn't give up her job just like that. Nonetheless, as Olga descended from the 25th floor, she was left intrigued by the man she'd talked with until past midnight. The meeting ruined her New Year holiday abroad: "I couldn't stop thinking about what I should do next", Kanovich recalled.

Immediately after the holidays, Gref heard that his offer had once again been rejected. He was annoyed, but gave Olga one last chance, along with his mobile phone number and three days to weigh up her options. The advantages — the chance to be part of the rejuvenation of a large and venerable Russian bank — eventually outweighed any doubts. Twenty years on, she found herself back where she'd vowed never to set foot again. For her, it was like travelling back in time. It was as if the last 20 years of the IT revolution had passed Sberbank by. As before, it was all shuffling papers and 'doing the slips'. Her staff looked at her incredulously when she talked about the outside world — apparently, in many places people were getting by just fine without Sberbank. Those who valued their own time and convenience avoided Sberbank completely. For the current generation of customers, the world was divided into two halves — online and offline. For people used to the speed of the Internet, what did a bank whose technology lagged not ten but twenty years behind the present day really have to offer? How much time did the older generation — which still held its savings books dear — still have left? And who would be left for all those thousands of clerks to serve?

It wouldn't be fair to accuse Kazmin's team of being unaware of the bank's backwardness. It was simply that the fear of botching restructuring the bank at the micro level — the day-to-day work of branch staff — was more potent than the arguments for change. One of the old guard had tried to warn Gref during a meeting in winter 2008: "You don't understand where you are! You don't understand that you can't touch it, you can't break it!"

"Why break anything? Everything works fine." The staff simply couldn't get on board with the vision

> "As my grandmother used to say, every house has its own way of creaking. If you always expect the worst from change, you're as well staying home and bolting the door."
>
> Interview with German Gref, Forbes Kazakhstan (11.2011).

Gref was trying to share. The man in the street, while no great lover of Sberbank, furrowed his brow: wasn't the devil you know better? People weren't willing to sacrifice the established order for the sake of nebulous and often unfathomable goals, even when that order appeared archaic and, at times, downright ludicrous.

Year on year, every evening without fail, every single branch of Sberbank carried out the same procedure simply because the Central Bank had once suggested it might be a good idea. The operation was known as "ordering by 20 digits". All documents that had been processed by the branch staff over the course of the day were organised in descended order according to the 20-digit bank account number they related to. This procedure wasted at least two hours of the working day, and took place in the evening, when everyone was ready to drop from tiredness and thoughts had turned to getting home to dinner and bed. Any actual value the operation had was debatable at best. Ostensibly, it was done so that any document that required revision was easy to find, clearly a rare occurrence. Day after day, hundreds of thousands of man-hours turned to dust that gathered on those carefully ordered files. The Central Bank didn't retract the recommendation, but Sberbank put a stop to the preposterous practice regardless, having never been a statutory requirement.

It was regarded as Kanovich's responsibility to reorganise operations. She disagreed — there was no formal operational division to reorganise. From her point of view, there was nothing to suggest that operational client support ran on strict, standardised norms of operation. In this matter, amateurishness flourished at the bank. Gref himself had been acutely aware of it, and by his own admission was at first "very afraid of the operational side of the business". This superstitious fear of meddling with the back office disappeared as soon as it became apparent that, in reality, there was nothing there to reform. A system had to be designed from scratch, and quickly. Unless operations were centralised somehow, modern retail banking would remain a distant dream for Sberbank.

Why was it such a big deal? Kanovich replied with a question of her own: "Could you go to space on a horse and cart?" New bank products, quicker service times (even with the successes of lean), the new emphasis on the customer — all of this would be rendered academic unless the bank got it right behind the scenes. If customers didn't sense the changes themselves, then it cast doubt on the whole enterprise, since nothing undermined faith in the intended reforms quite like preserving the status quo when it came to the customer experience.

However, Gref now had the right woman for the job. Kanovich was beginning to get the hang of tinkering with bank procedures. Back in the 1990s, she'd learned about shared service centres (SSCs), rare in Russia at that time. These were organisations responsible for routine operations such as dealing with customer calls or bookkeeping services. They were utilised by both a range of smaller firms, as well as large corporate networks and their subsidiaries and representatives. In this arrangement, it was more than a contract that connected the service provider to its user — the SSCs were formed and operated by the client companies themselves.

The history of SSCs in the US stretches back half a century. The first centres began to appear in the 1960s, after which they were picked up by General Electric and other industry giants. A couple of decades later, this wave of operational centralisation hit Europe. Kanovich remembered the project IBM developed for 86 agricultural banks in Spain. As individuals, each one had to bear the exorbitant costs of maintaining its own back office. This collective headache was virtually incurable, and promised to sooner or later push the banks to the brink of extinction. The SSCs came to the rescue, straightening out the banks' finances by circumventing these costly rituals. 86 banks had been represented by no less than 86 identical contact centres, bank card issuers and IT departments. The economy of scale of bringing together all this housekeeping reduced the cost of each and every procedure. The quality improved as well: even the most skilled craftsman is no match for machines and the conveyor belt when it comes to churning out generic products. Despite the apparent simplicity of the solution, SSC produced something of an industrial revolution in management.

Sberbank, with its vast network of offices, was in dire need of centralisation and, subsequently, its own SSCs. The first appeared appeared in Moscow and St Petersburg — 'Yuzhny Port' and 'Staropetergovsky' respectively. Sberbank bought up an entire business centre for its Moscow SSC, locating it in a converted paper-producing plant in the south of the city. The speed at which it was set up was incredible. Those that started at the newly opened centre did their best to work around the dust and noise of drilling. "We were motivated by a desire to get a lot done, and get it done quickly", said vice-chairman Stanislav Kuznetsov, recalling the prevailing enthusiasm of the time. Kanovich named each centre, and was careful about it. The same was done in the West to avoid suggestions that the service provider and the client company were a little too chummy. At Sberbank, this task took on particular significance. Kanovich felt it extremely important that service centre staff worked for Sberbank as a federated company rather than simply departments of any of the regional Sberbanks. If you want your products to be as homogeneous as a Big Mac — of identical quality and production time — regional variation is not to be encouraged. She even banned any suggestion that the centres belonged to the regional banks in internal communication: "I said, 'If I see anything of the sort, I'll kill you'".

Overnight, 800 Sberbank back offices dissolved into 15 SSCs. Even after this, the centralisation process was not complete. The next step was to consolidate these in five or six. These giant centres would finally be free of the risk of becoming appendages to territories in the strict administrative hierarchy. Kanovich was sure it could only improve the quality of the SSCs' work. The SSC was a machine for producing standard operations — it lived for instructions and algorithms, and cared not a jot for politics.

The SSCs took over hundreds of processes, from processing loan applications and claims to payments and currency exchange regulation. Even before the appearance of SSCs, there were plenty of people opposed to them in both Moscow and St Petersburg. With the opening of centres in Nizhny Novgorod, Yekaterinburg, Tyumen and Novosibirsk, the number of these detractors swelled. Immediately after Yuzhny Port opened, it became apparent that there was now a large surplus of personnel in the operational system, even before the centre was running at full capacity. Where before 38 people had been required for crediting funds to accounts, now 16 sufficed, and of the 99 staff members who dealt with issuing benefits and pensions, only seven remained.

> "We are the children of a nation where paternalism reigned for decades. Our employees have to learn to rely on themselves and trust that by changing themselves they change the world around them. This will take time. I'm not interested in working with an army of toy soldiers: such armies are only fit for board games."
>
> Interview with German Gref, *Komsomolskaya Pravda*. (02.12.2011).

"All our work has been taken off us and handed to the SSCs. We're all for the chop", accounts departments wailed fearfully. In the Urals, one in two of the poor unfortunates who were laid off were accountants.

Fear of redundancy mingled with resentment: experience no longer counted as a measure of ability, as the centres were inundated with youngsters. "The centres have just taken on tram drivers and whoever else replied to the ads. It's taking hours, sometimes days, to work out what they've done and then fix it", complained one representative of the old school. "They're just taking people in off the street", grumbled a member of staff at the Urals centre. "Where are they supposed to find 1,500 qualified workers?" In a moment of candour, a worker at Yuzhny Port wrote that she had to help out another office "at her own risk", since colleagues couldn't cope with the extra workload. "We handed over all the records to the SSCs, and now what?" was the complaint in the branches. "Total chaos when opening accounts, documents going missing all the time."

The first SSCs functioned as the glittering façade of reform. Special guests were shown round the arsenal of state-of-the-art equipment. It was here that Gref brought President Medvedev, impressing on him the ability of the newly kitted-out office to handle up to 2.5 million transactions per day. The bosses at Yuzhny Port proudly reported to Duma deputy speaker Vladimir Zhirinovsky during his tour the reduction of pension payment and salary processing from four days to four hours. Branch personnel looked on unmoved. They cursed their superiors for their voluntarism and the lack of respect shown to experienced staff. The line separating the back office from the retail staff increasingly resembled a battlefront. Communication between the two took place through gritted teeth, and they ignored each other's requests and enquiries. A shared hostility towards the radical transformations taking place at the bank fuelled the atmosphere of conflict. Arguing that it was just a matter of getting used to the technology fell on deaf ears: many staff had come to the conclusion that the standard of customer service was actually going downhill.

Kanovich put these strong reactions down to professional jealousy. She compared it to a housewife who had lost control of how everything was arranged in her own home. It was the kind of thing that might happen after moving house, when years of precious order is turned on its head. Something similar was happening to the branch personnel. Familiar procedure, honed over years of experience, was now in someone else's hands. Loose paper and stationery began to disappear from the desks as paperwork sharply decreased. There was particular outrage over the fact that the new online approach had made much of the interaction between customers and staff as visible to their bosses as the clerks' tears of frustration. Kanovich couldn't hide her sense of triumph. "They felt it was their domain, but it's ours now. I just took the key from them and looked through all their drawers."

One of the most problematic 'drawers' was unquestionably the credit process. For years it had been hidden behind a wall of outdated regulations while, even worse, billions of roubles of overdue loans lay in stasis. The terms under which they'd been issued were enough to put even experienced bankers into a funk. The situation needed to be dealt with, and soon.

CHAPTER 10
THE BILLION-DOLLAR SWINDLE

IT HAD BEEN ANDREI KAZMIN'S DREAM TO MAKE millions of borrowers out of the millions of depositors. One small detail remained: to work out how to offer credit at least half as simply and swiftly as other banks could. Alas, the chances of customers having credit approved, and the length of time for such approval to be granted, had fallen short of forecasts. The main issue was the completely unfathomable way applicants' creditworthiness was assessed. Deputy chairman of Moscow Sberbank Vasily Pozdyshev, who had made his career working at French banks, christened it the "banking Stone Age": "And to think, at Sberbank they call it risk management!", he said, puzzled. He saw nothing of the kind. Credit was granted or refused on the whim of branch loan committees. The only thing that had been centralised was printing out the guidelines.

Lending discipline, which Kazmin and Aleshkina had so heroically bolstered in the 1990s, managed to curb the worst of the embezzling. But later, the bank again found itself peering through its fingers in horror at how local administrations were issuing loans. The people who counted out bills and those who approved loans were working side by side in the same place. It opened the way for collusion with those of a less honest persuasion, even among the bank's security staff. The bank was sitting on a powder keg and nonchalantly lighting its cigarettes from the burning fuse.

Everything finally exploded in winter 2008. One of the bank's senior auditors reported that "compromised loan portfolios" made up half of the total in some branches. The bank's internal control service recorded a surge in loans approved using false documentation. Later, the details emerged. Major frauds had been discovered in three Moscow branches. Bank hold-ups, dishonest cash transit guards (such as those in Perm who'd snaffled 250 million roubles of Sberbank's money) and other criminal escapades were small fry compared to the Moscow fraudsters. Thanks to them, Sberbank's coffers were lighter to the tune of 35.4 billion roubles, an amount not far off the bank's net profits for 2009. Bosses there had been turning a blind eye to fake income certificates, and persons of dubious appearance and even more dubious backgrounds had been issued millions in loans. According to the newspaper *Vedomosti*, the capital's Lublinsky branch even had a priest from the ultra-nationalist Gotfsky Archdiocese of the Russian Catacomb Church among its apparent borrowers. Employees at head office whispered about so-called 'loan tours', where straw borrowers would allegedly be taken from branch to branch by the busload.

Gref disliked when anyone at the bank talked publicly about the thefts. The official press releases euphemistically described the Moscow branch loans as "high-risk". At a press conference, the head of Sberbank in Moscow, Maxim Poletaev, found himself having to laugh it off: "80% of arrears on retail loans, and 65% on loans to businesses are down to the criminal conduct of staff in the Lublinsky,

> "If Sberbank had been a person, Raskolnikov himself would certainly have had paid a visit at some point over the years. That can't be ignored either."
>
> Vladimir Putin's address at the Sberbank conference (12.11.2011).

Stromynsky and Meshchansky branches." When the crimes finally came to light, the independent directors were horrified: stealing more than $1 billion from shareholders?! And that's only from three branches in Moscow! How much had gone missing around the rest of the country?

Sberbank's own internal security repeatedly appealed to law enforcement agencies, but with no real success, as investigations were blocked by corrupt police officers. "We had hard facts, we knew who was involved and we had a breakdown of their criminal activities in the bank, but no criminal proceedings were initiated and no-one was arrested", recalled deputy chairman Stanislav Kuznetsov. Gref went to the interior minister at the time, Rashid Nurgaliyev, requesting he "commission experienced investigators to look into what happened". This got the case rolling, and ensured at least some of the fraudsters ended up in court.

After a period of time, a list of names appeared on the Sberbank website under the heading, "Employees dismissed from Sberbank". Virtually all had lost their jobs on the grounds of violating an article of the Russian labour code on loss of employer trust in staff members. The publication of this "black list" was accompanied by clarifications from the bank, which was acting "as part of ongoing efforts to increase transparency" and "to prevent potential illegal activities committed by employees and to increase client confidence".

The costs of the old system of lending did not run to the billions that had been pilfered. No one had thought it necessary to keep records of processed applications. The bank genuinely had no idea which percentage of applications had been approved and which had been rejected. Since nobody had taken much interest in keeping track of refusals, the management could not fully assess the quality of its lending. Without a full statistical overview, data on arrears didn't offer much at all. It meant that senior managers didn't have a full picture of what was going on, and in that position they could hardly articulate their wishes to the regional offices of the bank.

One of the first things the new team wanted to do was to start making more use of one of the bank's natural advantages — a huge borrower base on which to ground its analysis. Gathering and evaluating data became centralised with the bank's creation of a 'Credit Factory'.

Sberbank's main risk assessor, Vadim Kulik, fiddled incessantly with his hair during the meeting, exasperated, continually shaping and reshaping the mop on his head. Working with risk was no good for the nerves. As the Russian police service rebranded itself, transforming from *Militsiya* (militia) to *Politsiya* (police), Kulik asked if the bank could spot the difference between a militiaman who was going on to become a policeman from one who wouldn't make the cut. "Do you know? No? You need to be able to make the distinction. These days, all state employees are taking out loans before they get laid off. They learned this during the financial crisis", explained Kulik.

The guiding principles of the Credit Factory were minimum decision-making time, and maximum automation. The task was to approve loans for responsible borrowers and refuse them for those who could not or would not pay them back. Two figures were key in this: 0.03 and 72. The first related to loans considered what international banks designated NPL 90+ (non-performance loans in default for 90 days or more). According to Kulik's data, about three in every 10,000 Credit Factory loans were in such a category. 72 was the percentage of loans that had been approved. These indicators were necessary in order to understand arrears figures. If 99 out of every 100 applicants were refused, then the bank could be arrears-free, but such a bank was unlikely to be successful in the lending market.

An average Russian bank had about four overdue loans and 60 approved. There is a big jump between 4 and 0.03% in arrears. Kulik argued that his data had been drawn from a typical customer pool — there had been no special cases used to make a point, and there was no need to. Sberbank customers had always been conscientious in this regard. Even in its past life (before the Moscow branch frauds), defaults stood at 2.9%. The next question lay in how this had been achieved. The most popular type of credit at Sberbank was guarantor loans. Surety was a reasonably reliable mechanism for regulating risk (which was why the new team decided not to do away with them, merely adding the option to repeatedly change guarantor). The downside to the system was its archaism, a kind of echo of the collective responsibility of the Soviet past. Surety worked wonderfully in the villages and small towns where everyone knew each other or was more or less related, but in the big cities it was far from ideal for borrowers, and were more a source of worry than anything else.

The capacity of the Factory in the area of the Yuzhny Port SSC was such that it was able to make around 35,000 decisions on a daily basis, mostly approvals, with the whole process taking around 37 hours on average. Before, the entire weight of the operation fell on the shoulders of credit inspectors, who would spend a long while preparing the application for assessment by the credit committee, working out a repayment schedule and writing up an agreement. Now the need for this level of expertise was greatly reduced.

Separating the sheep from the goats from the outset was now something the average clerk was capable of. According to the new rules, they were to determine whether the person in front of them was who he or she claimed to be. For this, the bank made use of data from a number of sources, including information provided by the Federal Migration Service. Clerks were also to make note of any distinguishing features, such as whether potential borrowers were tattooed. Apparently, Sberbank regarded having tattoos as adversely affecting a borrower's capacity to repay his loan. The bank began to photograph customers (the shots would prove useful when face recognition systems were launched) and analysed their handwriting on the off-chance that the same hand had signed documents at other banks with which Sberbank exchanged information. Management hoped that over time, technologies for assessing borrowers would be shaped into a usable interface that the retail bank could employ. Vadim Kulik wanted the system to be a kind of ready reckoner for flagging up when suspicious or inconsistent data was entered, prompting further steps if required.

After confirming the customer's identity and completing all the necessary forms, the application would then be moved on to the 'Factory'. Here, the applicant was assessed on a range of different parameters, from the demographic (sex, age, marital status) to the behavioural. These indicated how different people conducted themselves when it came to repayments: how often and for which type of loans customers had applied, and whether these had been for example cleared early, or with frequent but minor overdue payments. The automated system took information from a number of different data sources. The first was credit bureaux — when they'd first appeared in Russia, Sberbank launched its own in-house service. The bank considered its data more valuable than other banks, and was not prepared to share it. Only with the arrival of the new team did the bank stop behaving like a dog in a manger, and began to offer data to independent credit bureaux as well as to use them as sources for information on borrowers from other market players.

Sberbank made active use of information gleaned from the Russian Pension Fund and the Federal Tax Service. It is hard to overstate the importance of this, as now the bank had access to official figures on salaries and unpaid taxes and could now, for example, identify the fly-by-night companies that produced the false income certificates for applicants who had little chance of being approved, and made no contributions to the Pension Fund. The bank has never named all its sources. However, it is safe to say that Sberbank had more access to information on individuals than any other Russian and, in all probability, Western bank had. And what did this indicate? It is fair to say that Sberbank had gained yet another advantage over the market by exploiting its status as a state-owned bank. Sberbank itself preferred to posit it not in terms of preferential treatment, but by presenting itself as pioneer — who else was going to lead the way and get moving with developing systems of information exchange? Later, VTB would go down the same route, and other major Russian banks followed suit.

> "I look to the way we were four years ago from today's perspective and I can see that at that time we had no risk management system as such."
>
> Interview with German Gref, Forbes Kazakhstan (11.2011).

CHAPTER 10 · THE BILLION-DOLLAR SWINDLE

It was not only individuals the bank now lent to in this new way. According to Kulik, corporate borrowing also experienced a complete shake-up. Not long before, the bank had had no consistent framework for managing risk, no transparent system of setting limits, and no IT support up to the task. A huge number of lending regulations were in place at every level in the hierarchy, but these rules were riddled with loopholes. Businesses were classified using a ranking system comprising six possible categories, only two of which were ever used — the biggest risks and the smallest risks. The world was divided into black and white. Kulik explained that proper evaluation procedures were circumvented — with one decision from the top, a company could move from the worst category to the best, and vice versa. The system's weaknesses were shown up when it came to groups of affiliated borrowers. Businesses borrowed "as much as they could carry" from Sberbank, and later often overborrowed. The bank made huge losses going down this path of corporate lending. The ease with which some companies were approved loans contrasted with the agonising suspense in which others were kept before decisions were taken. For the majority, the whole process was shrouded in an impenetrable veil of mystery.

First of all, the bank eliminated the discrepancies in the way risk was understood, and the rules that governed its evaluation. Credit transactions were now conducted on the basis of evaluations subject to uniform standards, and lending limits were also made consistent (unless they related to project financing). The client base was re-ranked according to 26 levels of risk, as opposed to the previous six, and the procedure for coming to decisions on granting loans was significantly simplified. Consultants from Oliver Wyman developed a more lightweight version of the credit committee. At Sberbank, it earned the nickname "the six-eye system". Three people would now decide the fate of loan applications: the client account manager, a credit advisor and an underwriter. The client only received the money when all three endorsed the application. With the underwriter given something like 48 hours to assess any potential risk, prolonged deliberation over decisions was eliminated.

CHAPTER 11
I'LL BE MAKING A COMPLAINT

AT THE DOORS OF AN ORDINARY BRANCH OF SBERBANK, customers lined up patiently for the staff lunch break to come to an end (the universal lunch hour was yet to be abolished). They shrank from the cold and glanced irritably at their watches. When the hour was over, they started forward — a staff member had come to the door, shoved a key in the keyhole and turned it a couple of times. This usually acted as an invitation to come inside. But the door didn't budge — it had jammed. The angry customers began knocking, before trying to force it themselves. When it eventually succumbed to their efforts, another unpleasant surprise awaited: bored clerks sitting at their windows, wholly indifferent to what had taken place in front of them.

This was an insult. A voice threatened to report them to their superiors. "I'll be making a complaint!" This typically Soviet reaction to a conflict situation seemed impotent at Sberbank. Was there any guarantee the staff's superiors would have anything to do with the matter? This time, however, the customer's complaint was heard. The manager of the branch with the temperamental lock was fired for her attitude.

Nonetheless, it was another reminder to Gref's team of exactly what they were dealing with. Retraining employees was a difficult task, but an increasingly urgent one. How to go about it?

Gref was a firm believer in the healing power of reading. His preference was for books on business practice. The Sberbank boss endeavoured to get through 300 pages a month, and claimed he often managed double that. For someone with his schedule, this was no mean feat. He had developed this interest in business literature while still in the employ of the state: "It was well known that he loved reading about new systems of and approaches to management", said Alexander Idrisov of Strategy Partners. "If Gref liked an idea, he tried to share it with others. He had his colleagues read the same books so that they were all on the same page." Sberbank vice chairman Stanislav Kuznetsov, who had worked with Gref for six years in the ministry, recalled how keen he was to share with colleagues the things he'd gleaned from his reading. He was so transfixed with the subject of modern management that he'd even bring it up at cabinet meetings.

At Sberbank, Gref's passion didn't wane. Vice chairman Bella Zlatkis would receive earnestly worded reading recommendations from the boss from time to time. Links to interesting articles in newspapers and magazines flooded her inbox. "I love reading myself, and assumed it was impossible for anyone to read more than I did. Gref disabused me of this notion", she admitted.

Impressionable by nature, he literally managed 'by the book', in itself a highly unusual manifestation of the business style that marked the Sberbank head out from the vast majority of his colleagues at the bigger Russian companies. Eventually, senior vice-presidents Viktor Orlovsky and Denis Bugrov had to give their boss a dose of reality. The amount they had to do, as well as the time they had to do it in,

> "I have the classic complex of someone who lacks education. I studied hard, and well, got an honours degree, but I still have that complex."
>
> Interview with German Gref, *RBK* magazine (03.2011).

CHAPTER 11 • I'LL BE MAKING A COMPLAINT

was beyond what was reasonable. It made their heads spin — they wanted to get a good night's sleep, and to spend weekends at home from time to time. Perhaps it was time to reassess priorities. They couldn't do it all at once. In response, Gref presented his team with copies of *Chasing the Rabbit*, written by MIT professor and Toyota expert Steven Spear, who in his old-fashioned glasses and bow tie seemed more of Teddy Roosevelt's era than Barack Obama's. The book set out to explain how those market-leading "rabbits", the so-called "high-velocity" organisations, actually operated. Unlike the armchair experts who pontificated from a safe distance, Spear learned the secrets of success on the factory floor. He managed to get a temporary job at one of the 'Big Three' US car manufacturers, awkwardly wielding an impact wrench to drive in the bolts himself. At the training centre, he was inducted into the art of driving in screws at different angles. Spear's ordeal at Toyota itself only lasted six months. The author intersperses his account of the experience with a discussion about the origins of long-term leadership, which he attributes to a culture of knowledge-sharing within the companies. Gref fell in love with the book. "Read it, and then we can talk", he would say dryly. Bugrov, used to reading his iPad in traffic jams and on flights, praised Spear's work as "ideologically correct". Orlovksy listened to the audio version of *Chasing the Rabbit* on his morning jogs. He'd later tell a trade journal that "Sberbank is developing according to the very paradigm described in the book", and summarised the author's conclusions: "Leading companies, if they quickly break away from their competitors in a number of directions at once, become uncatchable. For the leaders, it means one thing — their strategy can't and shouldn't be based on development in one area alone, even if it is strategically the most important. (...) This approach is an unusual one for Russian business, and one that for us was neither obvious nor familiar at first."

Gref did not simply foist the book on his immediate circle. He was enough of an idealist to evangelise about the power of reading to the whole company, much of which was populated by thirty-something women who had enough to think about with their own households. "Read books! Read Japanese, European and American writers. Start with Toyota and other companies that lead the way in innovation", was his advice to the staff, for whom he organised a free virtual library. Here is a typical passage from one of Gref's missives: "The other day, I read *The Experience Economy*, by Joseph Pine and James Gilmore. According to the authors, there's a new economy emerging — an economy of experience, focused on consumer perceptions. It's exactly what we're going through! We need to become the directors and producers of our new services. We need to wow our audience — that is, our customers — by expanding their outlook and impressing them with what we have to offer."

Sberbank's boss was fond of describing books he read in his youth as "life-changing". One singled out for particular praise was *The 7 Habits of Highly Effective People* by Steven R. Covey (employees of the bank complained to me that they'd effectively been ordered to read the book). A long-time fan of Jim Collins, author of *Good to Great*, Gref was also wont to embellish lectures to students with quotes from his work. Even Gref's "teaching an elephant to dance" was a nod to the book *Who Says Elephants Can't Dance?*

by Lou Gerstner, which gave an account of his firm IBM's transformation.

But none was held in such high regard as Janelle Barlow and Claus Møller's *A Complaint is a Gift*. In one of his letters, Gref requested every employee of the bank to read it. "It is a unique source that indicates whether we really are creating value for our customers and what we need to change for our products and services to meet expectations", crowed Gref. "We must change our internal procedure to create a new atmosphere of understanding with regards to the concerns of our customers and employees." *A Complaint is a Gift* served as the basis for corporate training seminars and video lectures. Gref would recommend it to the bank's partners at any opportunity. Copies bound in the company livery (the book was published in Russian as part of the *Sberbank Library* series) found their way to a host of Russian businessmen and politicians. The audiobook version was given as a present to the president of Tatarstan, Rustam Minnikhanov.

In Tatarstan, the book became required reading for the entire Sberbank staff. "We made everyone read it, from branch managers to clerks", reported local bank boss Rushan Sakhbiev. "When I visit a particular branch, I always ask: 'Have you read this book?' If they haven't read it, or worse, if they've read it and don't remember any of it, then they're not our employee. It means they shouldn't be allowed to work with clients."

The book, written in the mid-'90s by a couple of Western management consultants, suddenly became a cult classic at the Russian state bank. Why? Because Barlow and Møller offered Sberbank a sure if winding road to improved service. As trite as it may sound, the dissatisfied customer is often the only person who will

> "I registered my complaints by phone, where they go on about how the call will be recorded to improve the quality of service, and I spoke to the manager. But in the end, they shrug their shoulders, smile sweetly and say something that amounts to 'Oh, well.'"
>
> Forum entry on Sberbank, habrahabr.ru (04.04.2011).

give you the truth about service at your company. But were there many willing to listen?

Management resolved to listen to any and all complaints. If customer satisfaction is to be guaranteed, then you need to make sure you live up to that guarantee. An investigations service appeared, something utterly unheard of under Kazmin. Back then, you needed to be acquainted with a member of management, preferably no lower than a branch manager, to get even as much as a reply to your complaint. "The usual Soviet clientelism ruled in the bank", said Olga Kanovich. "If you had connections: problem solved. If not, you'd need to fight tooth and nail for anyone to listen to you." Gref, on the other hand, considered such indifference unacceptable and attributed it to lingering Soviet attitudes. It was apparent that the bank, which seemed to have an attitude to clients similar to that of soldiers to lice, bore no resemblance to the service company it aspired to be. Sberbank's president urged employees "to focus on the customer and his needs", but added sadly that "this is a problem for us, because we grew up in a different society. Traditionally, we've not been particularly inclined to respect individuality and personal interests."

Attempts by customers of the old Sberbank to register complaints with the hapless branches by phone or to write letters to the administration had proven equally fruitless. Under the old regime, many simply poured their resentment into the complaints and suggestions boxes, but even the most naïve understood how little this was likely to achieve. The boxes were often hidden from management, and sometimes from the customers themselves (I personally witnessed this happening in branches more than once). Now

"In one of the *Buttermilk Village* cartoons, one of the main characters spends a lot of time trying to photograph some forest creature, and runs all over the place to get this picture. That kind of client focus can't help but inspire respect, but wasting time is unfortunate."

Good morning, Sberbank! Communiqué (07.2011).

these scribbled complaints became just one tributary in a veritable torrent. Customers could now contact a call-centre, something that under the previous management didn't exist in the accepted sense at all. People also began sending messages directly to the bank's website. In 2009, a section boldly titled 'Sberbank against corruption' also appeared on the site for a while, designed to make it easier for people to submit complaints. With the launch of the SSCs, claims went straight to the investigations department. There, the whole transaction would be examined and a decision on whether to investigate taken on merit. The whole process was to take no more than 30 days, though head office assured me that in four out of five cases, one working week sufficed.

Complaints and claims were not only submitted along official channels. Passions ran high online as well, so Sberbank saw fit to put this unadulterated wealth of information to good use, something that other companies were often unwilling to do. In the Public Relations Office, nestled in the depths of head office, a sub-department sensitively titled the 'Customer Care Service' appeared. When they started they were assessing 300 complaints per day. The raw material for these was plucked from online forums and social networks by an external partner who trawled the internet for references to the bank. When the authors of these online tirades could be identified and contacted, the particulars of the case were clarified and a formal claim submitted to trigger an investigation.

The project was noteworthy for the make-up of the team alone — the average age of its members did not exceed 30, and it was fair to assume that these youngsters had spent a significant proportion of their waking lives online. Nonetheless, at least one member of the team was a former branch manager. In the old days, no one would have countenanced the idea of spending time and money engaging with nebulous world of social media. The bank's relationship with the internet was, in reality, hindered by its clumsy, impersonal website, and the Kazmin administration viewed the contents of blogs with no more concern than it would regard uncomplimentary graffiti on a toilet wall.

Sberbank's first major foray into the world of social media took place at the end of 2009. More than 7.3 million people, one sixth of the total user base, took part in its special New Year project *Svechi* on the social network Odnoklassniki.ru. This was a record-breaking number. "None of the brands in Russia got close to that level of participation", Nataliya Germanova, head of the bank's marketing department, proudly reported. The bank's campaign on another Russian social networking site, Vkontakte, was equally successful, becoming the largest in the popular site's four-year history, as users enthusiastically sent each other virtual gifts. Sending presents on Odnoklassniki had usually required payment — this time, Sberbank covered the costs in full, and the service was free to users. As a result, the bank's outlays on online promotion increased 2,528% on the previous year.

The bank's new image, developed by advertising agencies, surprised the online world, but could only go so far: online handling of customer service was a very particular challenge.

It was a time when the whole country was talking about Dmitri Medvedev's Twitter and Facebook posts, and social networks such as gosbook.ru and regionalochka.ru, designed specifically for government employees, seemed a faintly baffling

CHAPTER II • I'LL BE MAKING A COMPLAINT

novelty. The popularity of new media in Russia was undeniable. According to respected analytics company comScore, Russians were among the world leaders for internet use — as of 2009, Russian users spent on average 6.5 hours per month and viewed 1,300 pages on social networking sites. Sberbank's adventures were a popular subject for bloggers, from online non-entities to internet superstars. The popular blogger and media manager Anton Nosik was so affected by his experiences of the bank that he described them in some detail on his LiveJournal account: "If you want to know, it's not a bank at all," he concluded emphatically, "it's a museum where time has stopped. The people on Facebook up in head office just don't have a clue what it's like down there."

Gref didn't consider social media as a no-strings platform for promoting the bank. Its interactive nature meant that any of the beautiful illusions imagined in advertising could be quickly dispelled by any truthful (or, for that matter, false but convincing) comments online. It was, however, a simple enough job to find out what customers weren't happy with and indicate to them what steps you would take on this basis of this information.

A debit card is blocked straight after funds are credited to an account. After some phone calls to the branch and a little coaxing, the customer only gleans enough to know that an inexperienced clerk has accidentally credited the same sum to his account twice, but questions as to when his account will be accessible again are left hanging in the air. Sberbank staff promise to call back and keep him updated, but nothing is done. Another dissatisfied customer. Deprived of access to his money, he cancels a planned holiday. The forums of banki.ru, Russia's

> "An employed woman, 30-40 years old, with one child."
>
> How German Gref described Sberbank's ideal borrower in a meeting with Vladimir Putin during the summer of 2009.
> Interfax.

biggest 'complaints box' for bank customers, were full of stories like this. The majority were accompanied by a detailed description of events and required no further explanation. But often the basic information supplied amounted to little more than a frustrated howl (this was the internet, after all). That's where the sleuthing began.

"I hate Sberbank!" screamed the tweet. The bank was intrigued — what would compel someone to post something like this on Twitter? The bank tried to get in touch with the author of the tweet in order to establish the nature of the problem and help resolve it. As a rule, it didn't just condescend to placating every disgruntled customer (once they'd recovered the power of speech from the surprise of the bank contacting them at all), but actually encouraged every individual to state his case. The customer could then see that their exasperated cries had resonance, even when they were far from the standard mode of complaint. It spiralled from there. The growing number of complaints and claims, and the investigations that followed, encouraged people to seek recourse from Sberbank at Sberbank itself. Over two years, the total number of registered complaints, beginning from June 2010, increased almost 13 times, to 229,000. Almost exactly half of them related to the standard of service, and 48% of customer claims indicated deficiencies in the operation of self-service devices.

That the bank was actively involved in resolving these minor conflicts clearly indicated that the changes at Sberbank had been more profound than many had imagined. From management's point of view, the main thing was that it was now able to form an unbiased idea of the standard of service on offer through the eyes of its clients, and as a result now

CHAPTER II • I'LL BE MAKING A COMPLAINT

had a better notion of what and where it needed to sharpen up and re-evaluate.

Of course, not everyone was willing to be a source of information. Barlow and Møller had identified a few different types of behaviour in disgruntled customers. The first was the 'passives' — they walk out in silence, taking the insult on the chin. Another was the 'irates', who prefer informal and emotive assessment to official complaints ("If you could have seen the way she was looking at me!"). Irates serve as an indispensable source of 'word-of-mouth' information — along with those Barlow and Møller called 'activists', they would make a complaint but, dissatisfied with the response, would (unlike 'voicers', another category of complainant) continue to spread negative information about the company.

Which type of customer presented the greatest challenge to Sberbank? It would make sense to presume the irates — after all, those who got a kick out of making a fuss were generally not very receptive to apologies. Moreover, they were not likely to rest until they'd made their friends, family and neighbours aware of the outrageous treatment they'd endured. Sberbank, on the other hand, thought differently — the real problem lay with the silent types, who exhibited no outward emotion when in all likelihood they were positively fizzing with fury on the inside. Unfortunately for Sberbank, this type of person was abundant in Russia. Some customers could shout and swear, but afterwards forget what all the fuss was about as, ultimately, they didn't really care. As the bank repeated time and again, it was easier to make a loyal customer from an 'irate' than it was from a 'passive'.

In its quest to win over even a small number of people, Sberbank was prepared to do something

> "Comrade Gref pleasantly surprised me. When he arrived, he asked to be taken to some out-of-the-way branch in the city. This turned out to be in the Yubileiny district, where, naturally, no-one expected him to turn up. Going into the bank, G tripped on some torn linoleum... and fell over! At the very scene of the crime (in the area where customers are served), a public dressing down of the managers began."
>
> Post on an unofficial Sberbank forum on sbforum.ru (11.2010).

breathtaking — it was going to open itself up not only to complaints, but also to advice from its customers. Why shouldn't the bank invite proposals on how to solve its many problems? Jeff Howe, journalist for American publication *Wired*, coined the term 'crowdsourcing' to describe this interaction between companies and online communities willing to share (rarely for personal gain) their thoughts on technologies and products. These communities would propose ideas for a new product and willingly serve as a platform for testing it. Companies such as Google, Proctor & Gamble and Dell have at various times utilised crowdsourcing. Thanks to its IdeaStorm resource, Dell received around 10,000 ideas from customers (not to mention 80,000 pieces of feedback). Sberbank decided not to hang around any longer — its first forays centred on looking for advice on how to improve the way it dealt with complaints. The bank rounded on habrahabr.ru, a general IT blog. A dedicated site was started for the most proactive customers. "We invite you to hear others and be heard!" was Gref's introduction on the main page, "and we are convinced that working like this, within a 'collective intellect', is the only way of leading us to a breakthrough in the future."

Constant customer feedback kept the staff on their toes. Management did not expect much success from leaving employees to get on with it by themselves. Each employee had to keep in mind that they were being watched and their work was being assessed. Forms appeared in the branches listing the names of the staff and inviting customers to assess the quality of service: all it took was a simple tick in a box next to one of the categories: 'excellent', 'good' or 'unsatisfactory'.

Of course, external monitoring was no substitute for internal review. At Vavilov Street, they wanted to know as much as possible about what was happening on the ground. Upper management's chances of slipping into the branches unnoticed was slim (Maxim Poletaev's guerilla expeditions in Irkutsk being the exception). Deputy chairman for retail Alexander Torbakhov's was often accompanied by such a large entourage that his visits weren't always as sudden as they could have been. The guest would allow himself to be driven towards where he'd be expected in order to "assess the claims of the managers", but on the way he'd consciously deviate from the route, descending with the whole delegation on the first Sberbank office he came across. "In both cases, the effect was generally predictable", said Torbakhov. "In the first instance, it'd be all polished floors and radiant smiles; in the second, panic and alarm bells, clerks rushing to clear things off the tables and the cashier frantically raising the shutters."

Getting a true picture of the standard of service became a mission for which the bank drafted an army of inspectors. Each of the 2,000 recruits was expected to carry out at least 20 inspections per month, with the rules requiring a monthly check for urban branches and quarterly ones for rural offices. That wasn't all. For every banking controller, there were now four 'mystery shoppers' tasked with providing detailed formal reports of the situation on the ground. Questionnaires made up for them by the bank read like a detective novel with elements of fantasy thrown in. The whodunnit component of the survey propelled the respondent through a series of sinuous questions seemingly designed to catch employees out. The desired response was when it entered the realms of fantasy — well trained, positive and customer-focused staff. Gref wouldn't accept anything less.

> "..rudeness from customers has become a 'gift', so it would seem."
>
> Post on Sberbank-related forum, banki.ru (04.03.2012).

These mystery shoppers, the eyes and ears of the new Sberbank, needed to provide detailed descriptions of their experiences. How many windows were operational? What was causing queues? Management was interested in the smallest details of service etiquette. Was the language staff used with customers appropriate and not too colloquial? The bank outlawed displays of slovenliness in dress and personal grooming, and eating, drinking and chewing gum at the workstation was forbidden. "Informal posture" (folded arms, for example) and personal phone calls also became behaviours unbefitting an employee of Sberbank.

Front desk staff (now reclassified as customer service specialists) were issued with service instructions, or, to put it another way, scripts, which precisely laid out what to do in the presence of customers, and in what order. First off was the obligatory greeting, which required a polite "Good day" instead of a mumbled "Hello." They now needed to sign off with a "Goodbye" and a smile, something that in the West was mandatory as work uniform. In Russia, smiles had to be dragged out of service workers. "SPS got it out of us", lamented a clerk called Oksana on one of the bank forums. "Come on, work, smile like the village idiot who says hello to every Tom, Dick and Harry. But sometimes you just want to LOSE IT (sic!) at customers to get them to give their stupid questions about benefits a rest."

There were tens of thousands of such Oksanas all over the country. They epitomised the Sberbank of old. But it was just these types who needed to be dragged into the customer-centric world upper management was calling for. It seemed a hopeless task.

CHAPTER 12
DENIAL, ANGER, BARGAINING, DEPRESSION AND ACCEPTANCE

IT WAS ONCE FASHIONABLE IN THE WEST TO USE modern psychology to explain the logic behind managing change: how does a person feel when change intrudes into his familiar, predictable world? Get an insight into his reaction, and perhaps you can make the transition from the old to the new in business less painfully.

The renowned US family psychologist Virginia Satir, who studied how people experience changes in their lives, called them 'foreign elements'. These elements could just as easily include the arrival of a new company president with far-reaching plans for reform as a rift between spouses or a serious illness. As odd as it may seem, these examples do share one thing in common: they all deprive the sufferers of peace of mind. They begin to experience confusion and distress from the feeling that the ground is opening up beneath them. Chaos reigns in their lives. This painful phase of change is, according to Satir, unavoidable. But sooner or later it comes to an end, and the person's inner world comes into harmony with the outside one. He begins to adapt, to rethink his past and more easily accept the present.

The model, described by Elisabeth Kübler-Ross in her book *On Death and Dying*, published in the late 1960s, not only became a classic text of psychology, but also recommended reading for students of change management. While Kübler-Ross studied terminally ill patients, the findings of her work were also of interest to management experts. The Kübler-Ross model identified five emotional stages a person went through when facing the inevitable: denial, anger, bargaining (what can I do to undo events?), depression and, finally, acceptance. Employees in companies undergoing difficult transitional periods experienced similar feelings, albeit not necessarily in that order and, of course, in less dramatic circumstances.

There is some sense in diagnosing reform in this way. For most people, change, no matter how well intended, is bad news. For the average Russian, the perception is doubly negative: any reform is a step backwards, a ploy to take what little he has. The older generation had, for the most part, no faith in anything. The reforms that had taken place in the country had brought nothing to their lives other than grim fatalism and fatigue. They looked to the future not with hope, but with constant suspicion. During a phone-in with bank staff, Gref acknowledged that a third of employees were "against everything on principle": "These are people who don't see any transformation at the bank, who believe that nothing has changed, or that it's got worse, not better."

Gref invited political strategist and psychotherapist Alexei Sitnikov, with whom he had a passing acquaintance, to help with the problem. The had only met once, in St Petersburg over ten years previously, but Gref was won over by some gushing references. Sitnikov had been called "the greatest shrink in the country." At Sberbank, the wiry 50-year-old, noted for his casual dress sense, became Gref's advisor on communications and corporate ideology.

CHAPTER 12 • DENIAL, ANGER, BARGAINING...

At the end of the Soviet era, this native of Novosibirsk had wound up in sunny California. He studied there under John Grinder, the US linguist and psychologist, and the co-author of the concept of neurolinguistic programming (NLP). Grinder had had a huge influence on the Soviet student. Emerging in the 1970s, this new direction in psychology claimed to unlock the mysteries of human behaviour and thinking. Its creators stated that they were exploring "the structure of subjective experience." They were interested in how people experienced and constructed their realities. The Western academic community was not receptive to the new system and continue to regard it as a pseudoscience, while the most outspoken critics of neurolinguistic techniques see them as a cross between hypnosis and shamanism. However, in the Soviet Union, NLP went down a storm. Grinder subsequently paid tribute to his Russian student: unlike in the US, every psychotherapist in Russia came to know about NLP.

According to the Soviet system of education, which kept alive the spirit of Gustav Kirchhoff, there was nothing quite as practical as solid theory. There was an acute shortage of applied skills among psychology graduates. Sitnikov's course, one of the first in Russia, was continually successful. "More than 10,000 specialists have passed through me and my colleagues", he recalled. It was these students who would draw Sitnikov into politics a few years later. The consulting firm Alexei created in Novosibirsk, *Image-Contact*, became caught up in some stormy affairs. Sitnikov and his people helped politicians get elected in the CIS countries, eastern Europe and Latin America. "We took part in 410 campaigns, to be exact. We spent time in jail, we were wanted men, the lot. I think I'm still *persona non grata* in a

"I'm really into studying the psychology of human relations at the moment."

Interview with German Gref, *RBK* magazine (03.2011).

number of countries." Sitnikov shared his recollections in a cramped office, reminiscent of a solitary-confinement cell, hidden away among the labyrinth of floors in the bank's skyscraper. Some may view the Russian elections of the 1990s as largely farcical. Not Sitnikov — for him, they were an exciting intellectual adventure. The subject stirs in him a rather boastful desire to talk about the more colourful episodes of his career. Alexei had a hand in the creation of the party of the post-Soviet *nomenklatura*, Our Home — Russia, and took part in the 1996 presidential race, working in Boris Yeltsin's team and providing consulting services for his family. Afterwards, the demand for his services only increased. Among them were the young businessmen Dmitri Zelenin and Sergei Darkin, whose names would later develop firm associations with criminality (both would go on to win gubernatorial elections in Tver Oblast and Primorsky Krai in the early 2000s). However, his most daring project was undoubtedly the creation of the Unity Party, later renamed United Russia, which was led at that time by the seemingly incontestable pairing of Yuri Luzhkov and Evgeny Primakov. "We conducted psychosemantic research and an opinion poll representing every one of the 225 okrugs which encompassed 350,000 respondents. As a result, we found a niche for the new political project. For each constituency, we knew the type of candidate that could get elected there."

What was going on at Sberbank was a far cry from playing politics. Here, there was no electoral body, no parties, no political leaders with hackneyed slogans. But these technical differences didn't seem a concern to Sitnikov. He regarded himself as an expert in getting answers to the key questions from the depths of a collective consciousness. How to get people involved in reform, to make them stakeholders in the formation of a new company — this question, as Grinder's student realised for himself, was of greatest importance to his employer.

Sitnikov's first act was to travel around the country, meeting workers from the regional branches. Reflecting on life in the provinces and contrasting it with the agendas set at board meetings, which Sitnikov attended in an observational capacity, the consultant came to a depressing conclusion, further confirmed by the results of surveys conducted in the bank: the mindset of the management and that of the rank-and-file employees were in many ways diametrically opposed. Clerks had had the company's mission and values foisted upon them, and the new service culture forcibly instilled in them. Training had turned into duty. While meeting employees, Sitnikov had been bombarded with questions: "What do they take us for? Why won't they just let us work?" The motives of their distant superiors were regarded with typically Russian distrust. Many believed their reforms to be ill-conceived and destructive. The whole idea seemed to reflect the company bosses' excessive desire for privileges and wealth. Gref, who found such opinions unfair and inaccurate, couldn't simply push them to the back of his mind as he would a bad dream: "Be there alongside your people. Tell them that we're not just living it up, that we're just like them, working hard from morning until night, that we also despair of our failures and cheer our successes", were his words to one of the 50 managers he'd assembled under the transparent dome of Panorama, one of Kazan's most expensive restaurants (where a banquet was taking place in honour of *Sberbankiad*, part of a series of sporting competitions in which hundreds of employees from across the country competed).

The average earnings of management and regular personnel, even at the market's lowest ebb, differed by a factor of ten, and when taking into account remunerations for board members, by a factor of several hundred. "Sberbank spends billions of roubles on bonuses to senior managers": in a country where, according to Rosstat, the average monthly salary barely exceeded 22,000 roubles, this headline from *Komsomolskaya Pravda* couldn't fail to attract attention. Newsreaders explained to the populace that, on average, 70 million roubles was going to each of the 14 members of the bank's board. Reporters brandishing microphones conducted voxpops on the street, pouncing on passers-by with statements such as: "Six million roubles for a senior manager in the state bank every month! What do you make of that?" Earlier, a few hundred activists from the pro-Kremlin youth movement *Nashi* even staged a city-sanctioned picket at Sberbank's head office, demanding that the bankers voluntarily waive their bonuses, at least while the economy remained in flux.

No one was interested in what the management of big commercial banks was earning. Senior managers' salaries at Sberbank were not especially generous in comparison to the sums which those in similar positions in private companies were used to. The contrast was particularly striking at the outset of the reforms. "The former salaries of my colleagues were, in general, many times more than what they were offered here", Gref claimed. They wouldn't catch up with what private banks were offering over the next three years. In spring 2011, board members' remuneration was evaluated as being significantly lower than market levels. The pay of Sberbank's president himself was by no means excessive either: his yearly salary (excluding

---

"This issue of bankers' bonuses is being slightly overcooked just because Western bankers are, to put it simply, fat cats, and went too far, and so on... To be honest, it doesn't really apply to Russia to the same extent."

From Anton Karamzin's appearance on *Ekho Moskvy* (01.02.2011).

bonuses) barely stretched to the price of an average apartment in a Moscow new-build. "I suppose, by nature, I'm not focused on personal income", Gref mused to his employees. "Otherwise I could have got a different job, where I'd get a lot more for doing less."

Naturally, working for a stingy but demanding employer was not everyone's idea of a dream job. Year after year of 14- to 15-hour days and six-day weeks? For what? When, in early May 2010, Sberbank's 37-year-old deputy chairman Dmitri Davydov succumbed to cancer, the position of retail director was left vacant until the end of September. The main contender for the position, Alexander Torbakhov, who had resigned from his post as CEO of mobile operator VimpelCom in June, dallied on his decision. A couple of years later, he told me he'd been pretty worn out and allowed himself a proper summer holiday with his family. Moreover, he had every reason to delay making a quick decision on a new job, given the failures in his last. Sberbank hired the agency Top Contact, whose partner, Artur Shamilov, spent four months talking him round. The headhunter admitted to me that the remuneration amount, modest by market standards, was one of the obstacles for Torbakhov, but not the main one. "He was more interested in enterprises of a national scale. The money was secondary. Senior managers at this level were setting themselves and their children up for their whole lives. Perhaps they didn't have the private jets, but at the same time, they'd already made enough to get houses in Rublyovka."

The incentive system adopted by the bank lost out to the market in other ways too. The management's earnings were made up of fixed salaries and bonuses tied to annual profits. This guaranteed that the board would maintain a personal interest in good financial results, but only within fiscal periods. Such a scheme did not encourage working for long-term goals. In other words, the bank lacked a stock options plan. Growing dissatisfaction with the situation was regularly brought to the attention of the Central Bank. The state, reluctant to approve the plan, dragged out the matter as much as it could, something that infuriated Sberbank's management. Bella Zlatkis's face, normally set in a smile, would cloud over whenever anyone mentioned the subject in her presence. Even Gref did not hide his irritation: "We have invested, and continue to invest, a huge amount of effort and money in putting together a team — we take the best people on the market, train them, cultivate top-class senior managers, and then they're bought on the open market for two to three times the amount we can afford to pay", he complained in an interview with *Kommersant*.

It was difficult to suspect that Sberbank was unaware of what it was asking for, seeing that the man who'd introduced the first stock options plan in the country had joined the board. Sergey Gorkov, the head of the HR Policy Department, asserted that he'd done just that at Yukos as far back as 2001, when he'd been responsible for the oil company's HR policy. Since then, other members of the Russian business world had given such plans a try. However, Sberbank's main shareholder displayed a cautiousness that bordered on distrust.

An option plan is an instrument for rewarding management for its efforts: a manager is granted the right to buy shares at a fixed price at a given point down the line (three years later, for example). The difference between the current price and future share valuations thus becomes a matter of personal interest to the manager, but only as long as he remains with the company: leaving means losing his option, and therefore the chance to earn big bucks selling the shares on.

It all came down to money, ultimately — what else? This was something every employee understood. The message, reading between the lines on the multitude of discussions dedicated to the thorny subject of wages, was: pay us properly, and we'll swallow any pill, no matter how bitter. Management made no attempt to pretend it wasn't aware of the problem. But, in all its pronouncements, the bank indicated it did not intend to pay with equal generosity for the results of markedly different kinds of labour.

A clerk who had carried out a larger number of transactions could expect that his productivity would be reflected in a larger monthly bonus than his colleagues. However, quantitative motivation was no guarantee of quality — speed in serving clients did not eliminate indifferent or ill-mannered staff. Unusually for Russia, the bank began to train its managers to use behavioural methods for assessing their staff. Bonuses here were also tied to results, but quarterly now. The new '5+' system divided employees into five categories: "unsatisfactory", "needs to improve", "satisfactory", "excels" and "far exceeds expectations". Not friendly enough, motivated enough, productive enough? You only have yourself to blame. Independent, disciplined, but "not showing initiative to take on more work during a quiet period"? Not bad, but not great either. Demonstrating professional growth, "to a high degree independently", offering innovative ideas and anticipating the needs of the client? Take a bow. A similar five-point scale was used to evaluate whole branches. A bad worker in a poorly performing office had a coefficient of 0.1 against the basic bonus, while a star performer in a good branch scored 1.8. The difference was palpable: "All employees have a small fixed salary, but large bonuses are available, monthly, quarterly and yearly", Gref told state television.

The staff, believing they were being worked to exhaustion, were not especially cheered by this. They were increasingly convinced they were being used and that the bank was holding out on them. Many were sick to the back teeth of SPS and openly declared that more money was the only thing that would keep them at the company. How could this mindset be overcome?

Sitnikov believed the bank needed an ideology. Modern Russia had more than enough propaganda, but no ideology. This means of "seeing into the future, a system of values and appraisal, of heroes and anti-heroes" was as vital to Sberbank as oxygen, the consultant insisted. It was very important, he added, to explain to people what was happening in language they could understand, otherwise they could never share a common purpose. If Sberbank had no ideological underpinning, then weren't Gref and his team on equally shaky foundations? Sitnikov just shrugged: "The Chinese have a saying: 'The best time to plant a tree was 20 years ago. The second best time is right now.'"

But even the most elegantly devised and dazzling doctrine could not claim universal application. To overcome the prevailing mood, Sitnikov had no other prescription than methodically creating the conditions so that every employee enjoyed their job. He put it more simply: "It's a nice feeling to want to go to work in the morning, and get home in the evening." To Sitnikov, the fact that tens of thousands of its employees hated the bank was symptomatic of a common malady — an information vacuum.

"I need someone who can, for eight hours of the working day, whatever kind of mood they are in on the way to the office, treat dealing with clients as a pleasure, not a problem, because this is profitable for the company and for themselves."

Interview with German Gref, *RBK* magazine (03.2011).

In part, this was the trouble with being an oversized company in the largest country on Earth. Moscow's word was received in Kaliningrad, Murmansk and Vladivostok like signals from space. In an organisation that spanned nine (previously 11) different time zones, communication was always going to be an issue. While management in Sberbank's regional offices conferred with Moscow via video link, according to Sitnikov over 100,000 employees didn't even have access to email. The ideologically charged "Good morning, Sberbank!" messages, by which head office communicated daily with staff, were seen by only half of their potential recipients, and were likely read by even fewer.

Sitnikov worried that by forcing SPS and lean onto older employees — some of its most qualified personnel — the bank risked losing its "bridge over the transitional period". Why not show a little more flexibility when it came to personnel policy?

Stratification was seen as an alternative to this blanket approach. It seemed sensible to divide workers according to age, experience, professional expertise and career prospects. Sitnikov considered it vital to make a distinction between energetic young careerists and older clerks who wanted to be left to see out their days peacefully until retirement.

Sitnikov recommended more communication with employees, but did not consider this a cure-all. "All of us are like children who are persuaded more by the actions of our parents than their words", he remarked, while leafing through Adele Faber and Elaine Mazlish's *How to Talk So Kids Can Learn*. He, for example, couldn't neatly explain to a clerk who'd done her job honestly for years on end why she wasn't getting her long-service bonus, but was being rewarded for her innovation coefficient.

Meanwhile, comprehensive explanations were required for the hundreds of decisions taken by the bank, even those that seemed self-evident to the managers who made them. Nothing offers a more effective defence of reform than openness — it disarms the fiercest opponents and swells the ranks of those advocating change. It was not only Sberbank's workforce that was notable for its size: hundreds of thousands of shareholders were closely following events at the bank. As would become clear, they also wanted their say.

CHAPTER 13
COUNTING SHARES ON ONE HAND

36-YEAR-OLD LAWYER ALEXEI NAVALNY HAD MADE his name fighting corruption. Tens of thousands of people follow his LiveJournal, and he is regarded as the great hope of Russia's continually fractured opposition. But for management at corporations in which Navalny owned shares, he was primarily known as an activist shareholder.

Such people are familiar to anyone who has swum in the murky waters of corporate governance. In buying a symbolic stake in large companies, activist shareholders obtain the formal right to sway the actions of powerful corporate leaderships. Their motives differ greatly: some are concerned about the long-term growth of a company, while others are moved by more short-term goals. There is often a fine line between activist shareholders and greenmail vultures, who are little more than corporate extortionists. It was said of the renowned US shareholder rights activist and magnate Carl Icahn that he loved two things above all else: making money, and mocking management.

Activist shareholders would demand information on projects and deals that they believed may negatively affect shareholder returns. Hostilities commenced when information was covered up or their concerns not taken seriously, and they knew how to fight their corner.

They would pour out their indignation at any official event at which management was present. If necessary, they'd write angry letters to the regulators. Savvy in corporate law, they were prepared to sue, while publicising their actions as widely as possible. Naturally, they could always rely on the scandal-hungry business press for column inches dedicated to their crusades.

In 2007, the *Financial Times* compiled a list of the dozen most influential activist shareholders, mostly representing investment funds. Every one had at least one major conflict with big business to their name. They encompassed a wide spectrum, from British Energy and Arcelor to Cadbury Schweppes and McDonald's. Accountability to minority shareholders among European and US corporations usually amounted to little more than a declaration on paper. There, boards of directors were like members-only golf clubs. Yes, shareholder democracy was as venerable an ideal as freedom of speech, but in the West, just as in Russia, it was hard to imagine management prostrating itself to fulfil the demands of an insignificant minority shareholder, be they disclosing the details of a major deal or meting out severe punishment to those responsible for the previous financial year's poor results.

In Russia, where corporate ethics is an even more abstract concept than the independence of the judiciary, Navalny was in his element. He became, if not the first, then certainly the most conspicuous of the activist investors. Navalny acquired small stakes in companies such as Rosneft, Gazpromneft, TNK-BP, Surgutneftegas, Inter RAO, RusHydro, as well as VTB and Sberbank. This stern-eyed and sharp-tongued man earned a reputation as the Che Guevara of corporate governance, seemingly prepared

CHAPTER 13 · COUNTING SHARES ON ONE HAND

to question every rouble spent by the company on dubious objectives.

Navalny's tireless work cast a shadow over almost every major business either directly or indirectly connected to the state. The companies reciprocated his efforts, placing every conceivable obstacle in the way of his investigations. He was publicly called a crook and accused of shady dealings with Washington.

Kazmin's administration remained consistent: if the bank cared not a jot about its customers, why should its relationship with ordinary shareholders be any different? Whenever Bella Zlatkis asked for a response to the latest minority shareholder query, she was met with a shrug of the shoulders: "'Here's another one. You can count his shares on one hand.' The idea that this minority shareholder actually owns the company didn't enter anyone's mind," she recalls.

Samara had always been a special city for Sberbank, being where the majority of private shareholders were registered. Samarans had been some of the most active buyers during 'the people's IPO' of spring 2007 (a total of 30,000 people spent $526.9 million on Sberbank securities). But joy at this stable investment turned into disappointment within six months. The bank, at that time unwaveringly confident in its future, suddenly experienced a change in leadership. Some complained that the Samarans weren't even invited to the November 2007 extraordinary meeting (this is strenuously denied by Sberbank itself, which asserts that every one of the almost 200,000 shareholders had been informed in advance of the agenda and date of the meeting). Perhaps the real reason for the discontent was the lack of information about what was actually happening at the bank, but this was something shareholders were used to.

> "We as shareholders regard ourselves as owners of the bank."
>
> Interview with chairman of the Committee for Collaboration with Minority Shareholders of Sberbank Anton Danilov-Danilyan, In-house magazine *Pryamiye Investitsii* (05.2011).

Sberbank could be very pleased with its dizzying stock trends, but didn't consider it owed anything to minority shareholders. More respect, at least ostensibly, was shown for those with large stock holdings. Andrei Kazmin claimed to know them "by sight". They were, however, rarely to be seen at meetings, according to Kazmin. Assemblies under Kazmin were usually held in the spirit of party congresses. Not so much as a fly would dare buzz into the hall for fear of upsetting the sacred order. Honest dialogue was for the most part a myth. What problems were there to discuss, after all? Success was the only thing on the agenda.

For fellow participants in 'the people's IPO', Rosneft and VTB, whose securities dropped significantly after floatation, meetings were more democratic. Influential deputy prime minister and Rosneft board chairman Igor Sechin, who as a federal official was roundly demonised in the press, would openly engage with his audience. "Igor Sechin's demeanour at the Rosneft shareholder meeting did not did not conform to his reputation as the 'grey cardinal'", wrote *Vedomosti*. He both reassured and sympathised with minority shareholders angry at the drop in prices. Having to pay a deposit commission to Sberbank had done nothing to improve the mood (at that time, the bank was charging 0.08% of the market value of the securities per annum, and no less than 50 roubles per month, for holding the shares, and many shareholders were not prepared to make these payments). Several hundred people in the hall were aware that little depended on them, and the panel hoped that the hall understood this, but kept it to themselves. Yet the shareholders could not deny themselves the pleasure of taking big shots, these people desperate to give off a lordly air of control over markets, down a peg or two.

CHAPTER 13 · COUNTING SHARES ON ONE HAND

For uncomfortable, chastening questions and off-putting criticisms, few compared to Navalny, an "unusual" shareholder, as Rosneft's lawyers had put it. At a VTB meeting, he'd made an appeal to the supervisory board's conscience and reproached management for not doing enough to earn their salaries. Standing at the microphone, he painted a vivid picture: "These people sit with straight faces. A few even came here in cars with flashing lights. They are afraid. But the only way they can exist in this disgusting, corrupt system is through our silence. Don't be silent."

Was there anything for Sberbank's management to take from Navalny's eloquence? Yes, but surprisingly, the sparks from its clash with the fiery fighter for shareholders' rights left no residue. When Navalny was unable to ascertain the size of bonuses awarded to the president and members of the supervisory board, he went straight to the courts. According to Gref, he learned of this issue via the press. He provided the details of his contract to Navalny after receiving assurances that they wouldn't be offered as morsels for the delectation of the blogosphere. However, it hadn't been necessary to provide anything — Gref simply pointed the activist to a Moscow-based newspaper that had decided to make a pet project of his contract, it being the type of publication where no-one would expect to find reliable information on the earnings of the largest bank in the country's leading man. The conflict was snuffed out before it really got going. The numbers themselves didn't make much of an impression on the minority shareholders in any case: "I have a huge number of issues with Gref. We have quite an aggressive correspondence. But his large salary doesn't bother me particularly. It's an average salary, which compares to similar salaries in similar banks. That's not a problem", Navalny told *Ekho Moskvy*.

The quarter-billion dollar credit line offered by Sberbank to the Moscow School of Management Skolkovo would lead to investigations of a whole different calibre, and a scandal that would resonate much further. The business school was considered the largest education investment project in post-Soviet history, and the government took a particular interest in its completion. Skolkovo sat alongside an eponymous investment centre that sought to realise the Kremlin's dream of creating a Russian Silicon Valley. President Medvedev himself was head of the school's board of trustees. In these kinds of projects, it is not easy to separate business from politics, and any decision the bank took without demonstrating transparent market motives was like a red rag to Navalny.

In 2009, he had opposed allowing state corporation Rostec to manage problematic engineering assets ceded to Sberbank as debt. He had also disapproved of restructuring loans to workers of the crisis-hit Tver Carriage Works. Putin had petitioned Gref on behalf of workers after visiting the plant. "The workers are of course not to blame for anything, but the bank can't simply write off loans on one official's say so", was how Navalny explained his position. He had just as many questions pertaining to Skolkovo. Navalny couldn't understand what the bank had to gain from financing an educational institute "which clearly wouldn't bring in substantial profits in the foreseeable future." The terms of the loan were not disclosed, something that only increased his suspicion: non-market rates and a guarantee that in all likelihood amounted to no more than a spoken promise. "Alexei made an official

CHAPTER 13 • COUNTING SHARES ON ONE HAND

request for me to look into the situation surrounding the loan", said independent director Sergei Guriev. "I contacted management for clarification."

It took months of reminders before Gref took the time to write to Navalny. His letter explained nothing. It was a diplomatic but hollow response, and its central message boiled down to banking secrecy requiring the details of the deal to be withheld. Alexei valued the fact that the company's boss was giving attention to the matter, but was not satisfied with his explanation. Navalny expressed the essence of his position succinctly: "I believe that I am the bank. However, the bank believes that I'm not."

The story could have rumbled on *ad infinitum* had Skolkovo not switched lender, to Gazprombank. Sberbank was happy to wash its hands of the situation and get rid of the controversial loan, an act that was no less beneficial financially. Soon afterwards, with the borrower's consent, the bank revealed the terms of the deal, disclosing the interest rate as well as the way in which collateral and guarantees had been structured. There were no more secrets.

Usually, Navalny was extremely sparing in his praise of management at state companies, but for Sberbank he made an exception: "Gref has shown himself to be a good man", Alexei wrote on his blog. Moreover, he admitted that "in some respects, I was wrong — the interest on the Skolkovo loan was at market levels."

Why hadn't the bank simply brushed off this tiresome shareholder with his constant and, as it turned out, not always well-founded suspicions? After all, this was precisely what Navalny's other charges were used to doing. And it's exactly what Sberbank would have done two to three years earlier.

"I've bought 100 shares in Sberbank on the market. Am I now a shareholder?"

V. Malikov, forumprobanki.ru (12.02.2012).

Anton Danilov-Danilyan, in charge of relations between the bank and minority shareholders, had proudly reported at the annual meeting that the notorious activist was acting unusually "amicably and constructively". Navalny was not only tolerated — he was valued as an independent observer. Suspect lending? Murky financial potential? It was clear that this "unusual" shareholder was willing to speak up at the merest doubt. "Sometimes you just want to say what a horrid chap this Navalny is", Bella Zlatkis admitted to me, "but for the bank, this kind of person is very useful." Gref agreed: "With us, Navalny is constructive."

I had heard a lot about the Sberbank president's earnest faith in communication and feedback. As his colleagues confirmed, Gref needed no convincing that open dialogue was the best way to avoid misunderstanding. In 2008, the bank set up a committee for cooperation with minority shareholders, which, along with others, Alexei Navalny joined (he had been unsuccessful in his attempt to be elected to the supervisory board, which as a rule required the support of no less than 2% of shareholders). For the first time, shareholders based in the provinces were able to communicate with Moscow via video-conferencing, and, occasionally, in person. Management were now required to attend committee meetings taking place in other cities around the country several times a year, giving local shareholders a chance to ask questions. A separate website and dedicated call centre were set up for minority shareholders, whose numbers had long been comparable to the number of employees working at the bank. This brought the bank markedly closer to international norms in terms of the standard of its dealings with shareholders. Back in 2006, while Kazmin

CHAPTER 13 • COUNTING SHARES ON ONE HAND

was still in charge, non-resident stockholding had accounted for at least 20% of the total. Subsequently, their share only increased. This wasn't exclusively Cypriot and Virgin Island offshores hiding the assets of Russian entrepreneurs; shares in the bank had also been snapped up by so-called qualified investors comprising hundreds of overseas funds.

Eventually, the annual general meeting of shareholders, held at the bank's head office, became a more open affair. Its audience was greatly expanded by the implementation of webcasting, and questions directed to the chairman of the board were never blocked. This was apparent from their content alone: "I do not consider myself a crook. I don't feel I should I apologise for anything or to anyone and am prepared to state my case on any question that may be of interest to you", Gref retorted at one meeting after an attack from the hall. Those hoping for a row or some public squabbling were wasting their time. It wasn't that the hall was short of people willing to test their vocal chords. It was simply that shareholders had no real reason for protest. The bank had clearly made progress. Market share, profits, dividends and market value were all growing, and rapidly. In a short time, Sberbank would take second place in a list of companies offering the best stock yields over the previous ten years (the top position was occupied by Apple). *The Economist* estimated that $100 invested in Sberbank in 2002 would yield $3,722 for the fortunate shareholder by 2012. Moreover, according to 2011 analysis conducted by Boston Consulting Group, the Russian state bank was the second most successful bank in the world for returns on assets, with a return on equity of 27.5%. Only Bank Rakyat Indonesia, another state-owned bank, did better at 34.8%.

Those listening to the confident speeches of management were the same people who had bid a sombre farewell to Andrei Kazmin in the last days of autumn 2007. Back then, the bank's new president had spoken of market signals and dancing elephants, but the hall hadn't been much in the mood for flowery imagery. The great bank had just been handed over to a dilettante: what would become of their shares now? But their gloom had turned to enthusiasm pretty quickly: shareholders started to believe that there was much to be gained from Gref's reforms. It was just a pity that the same couldn't be said for all the bank's employees.

CHAPTER 14
SPARE PEOPLE

FOR FORMER ALPHA BANK MANAGER NATALYA Karaseva, her first days at Sberbank were an unending culture shock: paper piling up on her desk at an alarming rate; people rushing around with an inconceivably long stream of documents for her to sign. The thought rushed through her head: "So this is what a bureaucratic hell looks like." Karaseva almost yearned for her old job, where they had long before moved over to electronic document processing.

The most interesting times lay ahead. It was time for the newly-appointed Director of Retail Lending to meet her subordinates. Karaseva was presented with a list of 52 names, most of whom were credit inspectors. Credit inspectors were people who worked directly with clients. What, then, were these people doing at head office?

Employees were simply not doing what they were supposed to, hence the confusion. Half of these specialists Natalya transferred to colleagues in other departments. The other half? Karaseva paused heavily: "In the space of a year, the 28 people I had became 17. Many of them had spent 15 years in the same place, doing the same job in the same way and had no desire for anything to change."

What was happening at head office was only the tip of the iceberg. Karaseva's 52 credit inspectors were a fraction of the number in the country as a whole. A wave of lay-offs was about to sweep the bank.

> "I need to resign as soon as possible, if I find somewhere else to go. After three years working at Sberbank, almost every day I'm ready to quit, but every time I thought that as soon as I go, they'll start paying out bonuses."
>
> Post on unofficial Sberbank forum, sbforum.ru (11.01.2010).

"By making Sberbank better, we have the chance to improve the lives of 270,000 people," wrote Gref in spring 2009 in his monthly letter to staff. However, for 60,000 workers, prospects weren't so rosy — retirement (not always on an entirely voluntary basis), or redundancy. According to the strategy, 214,000 employees were to remain at Sberbank by 2014. A decision was made to implement the plans gradually, reducing the personnel by 3-5% per year while increasing the number of transactions by 8-10%.

For Russia, these figures were unprecedented. Until then, not one state agency with staff numbers comparable to Sberbank had dared been the cause of unemployment. At Russian Post, where 415,000 people worked (0.5% of the nation's entire working population), the subject of lay-offs was not even broached. Rural post offices (70% of the total number) lost money hand over foot, but this didn't seem to matter a jot. Since 2005, on government insistence, Russian Post have implemented a moratorium on closures, and in 2006, increased staff salaries by an average of 42%. The growing prosperity of Russian postal workers was occurring during one of the most dramatic periods in the history of the worldwide postal industry, with electronic correspondence ruthlessly vying with traditional paper forms. In Germany, staff numbers at Deutsche Post almost halved from 399,000 to 225,000 people. Royal Mail in the UK was also in trouble, while in Sweden, post offices had been all but replaced by kiosks in supermarkets and car parks, all at the expense of staff numbers. Only in Russia were new vacancies opening up.

"Before, our rural branches worked three days a week and four hours a day; now, it's five days and eight hours respectively. Naturally, this requires increasing staff numbers to cover the full shift cycle", Igor Syrtsov, head of Russian Post, explained to me in October 2007. He treated with a dry irony the brilliant advice of the consultants to stop recruiting and make the existing staff do more. The extra attention Gref — then minister for economic development and trade — was showing to McKinsey's analysis brought a wry smile to his face. Subsequent events were to change this condescending attitude. By strange coincidence, Syrtsov was in calm discussions about the staffing situation three days before his sudden dismissal. The incoming director, Andrei Kazmin, didn't last long at Russian Post himself — just over a year later, he was gone too. Nevertheless, the frequent changes of leadership did not shake the foundations of the personnel policy at Russia's largest federal state unitary enterprise: undermining its social stability was a risk no one was willing to take.

Under the old regime, Sberbank had followed the same course. The organisational reform carried out by Kazmin and Aleshkina at the beginning of the 2000s before Gref's arrival was considered as big as it could get. The number of regional banks was reduced fourfold, and branch closures occurred in certain places. But the shake-up didn't seriously affect staff numbers — they decreased by 2% (in all, 4,028 people). Gref's team considered the size of the bank's workforce excessive, to put it mildly. It was bloated even by Soviet standards: in 1988, in the whole of the USSR, including the non-Russian republics, Sberbank employed 248,000 people. "Sberbank compensates for its professional and technological lag behind competitors by having more employees carrying out the same transactions," Gref had told these same employees a year after his appointment.

What did this mean in practice? By way of illustration, Irina Shvakman of McKinsey's Russian office pointed to the simplest of transactions — withdrawing money from an account. In Russian bank X, this required two people and five documents. In bank Y, the number of documents is reduced to two, but three employees worked on them. "But the regulator's requirements are the same", Shvakman stressed. "It's simply that that's the way it was done years ago and no-one got around to analysing the validity of these transactions." In US banks, a withdrawal was dealt with by one employee using three documents. The resulting transaction time: 1.6 minutes, compared to six and eight minutes for banks X and Y respectively.

Comparisons were unfavourable in many other respects as well. "For example, we looked at how many accountants we had within the overall workforce, and the volume of transactions here and at other banks, and saw that we have a clear over-abundance of people", recalled Valentin Mikhov. There was no question of what to do with the extra staff: it was time for Sberbank to bid them farewell.

This didn't follow the usual script of modernisation, Russian-style. Any factory worth its salt would immediately bring the full weight of government down at the merest mention of such plans. Governors, deputies and procurators didn't want to hear about large-scale cuts. Continuing inefficiency, low productivity — whatever, just no job losses. When, in 2009, the car giant AvtoVAZ's decision to make staffing optimisations hit the news, the administration was subjected to incredible pressure from politicians. Management was forced to abandon the idea, despite having already signed off on the redundancies of 5,000

"I know a family, neighbours of mine, the adults of which all work in the same branch, and do you think they're all literate and tech-savvy types with two degrees (or even just the one)? Of course not. I know for a fact that these people (the older ones excepted) all tried their luck at other banks but didn't make the cut, so are stuck working at Sberbank."

Post on forum discussing Sberbank, habrahabr.ru (13.02.2011).

workers. 5,000! Sberbank expected to make tens of thousands redundant. It was clear that Gref had been given carte blanche to act at his own discretion, paying little heed to the grievances of federal officials, and even less so to those of the regional elites.

However, forced redundancies didn't sit nicely with the new management's developmental ethic. This presented a serious moral quandary. Staff cuts were a betrayal of the Japanese canons that had so inspired Gref. Toyota, Matsushita and the other great corporations in the Land of the Rising Sun didn't lay anyone off (the sacking of 2,146 Toyota workers during an acute sales crisis and severe money shortage in 1950 led to a two-month strike, after which company president Kiichiro Toyoda resigned); their sense of corporate morality baulked against it. One of its basic principles stated: useful work can be found for any employee of the company. The duty of managers lay in making even the most modest contributions of human capital profitable. The subject of superfluous, unproductive people was a favourite of Grigory Fidelman, a pioneer of private insurance in Russia. In 1988, he was among those who founded ASKO, a company with a once big reputation and extensive national coverage. After 'divorcing' his partners, Fidelman went on to head reinsurance firm Moscow Re. Of everyone I spoke to, this keen-eyed, bustling man was perhaps the most avid fan of the Japanese style of management. At the start of the 2000s, he began to cultivate a culture of absolute loyalty among his staff. In the context of Russian business, this seemed incredible, but Fidelman worked resolutely towards his goal. The main thing, he explained to me after five years of running this experiment, was to allay the fear staff had of their employers. Only by eliminating the threat of repercussions could a great business be established. Customers would receive superior service, shareholders would get a high return on capital investment, and staff would be guaranteed a stable, prosperous future. Fidelman sought the managerial equivalent of the philosopher's stone. He was deeply taken with the ideas of W. Edwards Deming, the father of Japan's quality revolution. One of his commandments had particular resonance for Fidelman: employees are to blame for no more than 2% of a company's problems; the other 98% are failures of the system. The head of Moscow Re rejected imposing penalties on employees, and a deciding veto was applied to dismissals initiated by the employer. The firm's 80 employees essentially had jobs for life. However, in 2006, it all came to a sudden end with Fidelman's departure. The reinsurance firm's owner Kakha Bendukidze praised his humanist ideals, but had his own ideas about how to develop the business.

> "Banking is become an increasingly expensive activity. In the long term, banking margins will fall."
>
> Interview with German Gref, Forbes. (21.03.2012).

Moscow Re was a small, fledgling company. Sberbank was a crumbling empire. Fidelman knew each employee by name. The bank's board members saw hundreds of their colleagues in lifts and corridors on a daily basis, but barely knew half of them. Fidelman's passion had not kept him in a job. What did this say for Sberbank? Socialist approaches to staffing had played a cruel trick on the bank. Sooner or later, its staff would have to face up to the harsh realities of the market. Ten years earlier, Microsoft boss Bill Gates had questioned the need for banks to exist in their present form at all. Being encased in iron and surrounded by stone walls seemed an increasingly tenuous advantage in today's world. The British magazine *The Economist* once suggested to its readers that if competitive advantages took the form of objects that could be dropped on one's foot, then they strongly advised revising one's business strategy. The popularity of so-called 'direct banks', which did not operate any branch network, had grown around the world and, in more recent times, Russia as well. Only a telephone and Internet connection were required to access services. Sberbank had a network so large that the entire country was within walking distance of a branch, but sooner or later this leviathan would fit into a mobile phone or laptop no thicker than a sheet of plywood. Its extensive geographical presence and enormous workforce was still the bank's greatest resource, but for how long? As services went online — according to IT director Viktor Orlovsky, this applied to 90% of services at some Western banks, and Sberbank was moving in a similar direction — people and premises were destined to become burdensome. Management was encouraging hundreds of thousands of people to build a brighter future for themselves in a place where, in all likelihood, there was no room for them.

Painful lay-offs struck a discordant note against calls for staff to put their heart and soul into the bank's rejuvenation. Reducing the number of employees while simultaneously expanding the scope of work for those who remained inevitably led to their being overworked and stressed. According to Mikhov, the number of transactions a clerk was expected to perform increased by an average of 60%. The abbreviation SPS came to stand for "Self-Provoked Sacking" and "Sberbank's Poor Sods". Clerks in the Moscow branches complained that what had once been achieved over a normal working day now took three or four to get done, often required working late into the evening. The intensive programme of retraining and new service standards that were continually being amended by bosses all significantly complicated the lives of workers who had until then felt they had their trade down to a T. This hadn't included any spaghetti diagrams, takt times or five-minute brainstorming sessions. Their dissatisfaction spilled onto the Internet. Forum users vented their fury on management, pouring withering criticism onto the production system it had created. Despite the heightened tensions, there was little chance that this emotion would grow into something more. The online revolt was first and foremost driven by those in the larger cities. New means of communication hadn't quite reached the more far-flung of the provinces, and even in those places where the internet had stretched its tentacles, few people thought to share their woes with a computer monitor. The disconnection typical of employees of large companies was amplified by the huge distances, poor communication and dismal level of social emancipation.

Gref was a strong supporter of a corporate culture in which "people are not afraid to express their opinion". At the same time, he hated lazy generalisations about how awful everything was. "I can't stand those types of conversation", the Sberbank head admitted. He believed in the law of 'ten percent': "In any organisation, in any society, there is a core of the most active and independently-minded people who will not be silent." However, the rest preferred to keep a low profile. People were paralysed by an inherent terror of their superiors. Often, it took being sacked to overcome this, since there was nothing left to lose. The 'silent types' who had been no help in the bank's efforts to better understand its clients also prevailed among its own employees.

> "I'm afraid the only thing we can do is go on about how much it all sucks, that we're sick of it all, that they're walking all over us. But just going and staging a walkout? Sadly, we're just too weak!"
>
> Post on Sberbank-related forum, story-online.ru (21.10.2010).

CHAPTER 14 • SPARE PEOPLE

In such circumstances, organised protest remained little more than a theory. In other countries, banks and bank workers have shown they are capable of asserting their rights just as well as miners and air traffic controllers. Back in the '60s and '70s, Ireland's largest banks were rocked by one strike after another. These lasted so long — in all, about one year — that economists were let loose to conduct research into the viability of operating a modern economy without access to banking services (one of them, Antoin Murphy, came to the conclusion that in a country as small as Ireland, whose population at that time was around three million people, life could go on just fine without banks). Clerk revolts were a regular occurrence in Latin America. Approximately 400,000 bank workers in Brazil, acting through their union, demanded salary increases from the National Banking Federation (Fedraban). Staff in Israeli banks frequently went on strike to demand payment of bonuses and the renewal of collective agreements without change of conditions.

The traditional weakness of local unions prevented the same thing from happening in Russia. The only noted attempt to create an independent organisation was undertaken in 2007 by a former Citibank branch employee, Ilya Strokov. The banking group, whose overseas offices were already rolling up their sleeves to get to grips with the unfolding financial crisis, had intended to carry out staffing optimisation in Moscow. But the bank's leadership suddenly found itself confronted by resistance from one of its former managers, who had by this time already been dismissed for clashing with his immediate superiors. Strokov had been dissatisfied with Citibank's system of staff motivation and time-keeping, but primarily referenced the Labour Code, which essentially forbade employer-initiated dismissals without the prior agreement of the "relevant superior trade union body".

He went ahead and created this body himself, making sure to do it properly: it had an advocacy group, a members' assembly, an elected chairman and even joined the Union of State Workers and Public Services (which also counted the unions representing the presidential administration, federal government and Moscow mayoral office among its 140,000 members). But despite this, Citibank refused to come to the negotiating table. The bank's lawyers made every effort to convince the court to declare Strokov's union illegal. This conflict made a few waves, but essentially ended in stalemate.

As ineffectual as it had been, it was nonetheless difficult to imagine this kind of thing happening at Sberbank. Any trade union activity was kept strictly within limits defined by the bank's management. It had always been this way. Or at least it had been this way since 2000, when a loose-knit collection of trade union organisations across the country was brought together as a single entity. This association had been run by one of Sberbank's longest-serving employees, Galina Rybakova. Her loyalty to the bank had been proven beyond doubt over her years of service. Under Kazmin, she had joined the board and been issued 0.01% of the bank's ordinary stock (1,900 shares). In December 2006, with the share price at $2,999, Rybakova's stockholding came to a cool $5.68 million (she then sold most of it off, reducing her holding to 0.007% of authorised capital). With Gref's arrival, Rybakova became one of his advisors, combining this with her union duties. Could such a union still be considered independent? "One cannot live in society and be free from society", was Rybakova's classic Marxist-Leninist response.

As head of a union that covered 80% of a workforce several thousand strong, there was no need to look for conflict with the administration when there was none. On the contrary, Rybakova noted that the bank's bosses were making efforts to improve working conditions for their people. In autumn 2010, Sberbank concluded a new collective agreement with the trade union. Unlike before, union leaders now had the right to sit on board meetings of the regional banks. Union positions were, however, mostly represented by senior staff themselves — departmental heads and deputy chairmen. How was the 'party line' to be towed if they weren't in control of the situation? Rybakova seemed to be fine with this.

The bank expanded its social security provision, insuring its workers against serious illness and accidents, and also covered half the cost of private medical insurance. Included in the programme was, according to the official wording, an enhanced staff medical screening. For staff who underwent it, it was more reminiscent of an army medical, passing all those who were not blind, deaf or mute fit for service. This military order became established throughout the bank, but particularly in Moscow, which was destined to become the main testing ground for the new Sberbank.

"Where's our union? It exists, but it is run by the management, so it in no way stands up for employees' rights. Employees are actually afraid of reporting anything to such a union."

Forum post in 'Comments on working at Sberbank', www.banki.ru (20.05.2011).

CHAPTER 15
AN UNLUCKY NUMBER

THERE WERE FEW CITIES IN THE WORLD WHERE banks were crammed so tightly together. In 2008, the Association of Russian Banks estimated that financial retail coverage in Moscow was at least one and a half times greater than in London. In the British capital, there was one bank branch for every 5,300 people; in the Russian capital, it was one for every 3,520. But even in this money-mad city, there were some places that bucked the trend.

The Lublinskaya Street relief road, located on the outskirts of Moscow, was not a particularly busy stretch. Retailers hadn't bothered to assess the level of traffic along it — the woods around Moscow seemed busier. This was confirmed by the frequently changing signage above the local shops. One particularly optimistic entrepreneur had once tried to open a reasonably-priced, European-style bakery in this sleepy backwater — it didn't last a year. Nonetheless, there were some who took a fancy to this quiet Moscow street. Below the identikit high rises, the banks set up shop: MDM Bank, Uralsib, BTA Bank, Russian Standard and Renaissance Credit all established themselves on the strip. The sixth financial institution to stake its claim on the land was Sberbank. Unlike its neighbours, there was no lack of visitors there, even in the afternoon. People choosing to pay their bills at the more convenient moments of the day were often left standing on the street, propping up the

CHAPTER 15 · AN UNLUCKY NUMBER

back of the queue. But Sberbank's obvious popularity wasn't helping it make money.

Less than a third of the bank's branches in the capital were located within the Third Ring Road — the territory usually considered the furthest extent of Moscow's centre. The rest were spread about the city's outskirts. It should have been the other way around, Moscow's Sberbank head Maxim Poletaev told me. After his success in Siberia and the adrenalin rush of lean implementation, Poletaev was about to get started in the capital. He was like a sprint coach sent to teach marathon runners how to cover a few dozen kilometres in a couple of minutes. "Moscow has 2.5 times the income of the rest of Russia", he argued loudly in his office, the windows of which looked out onto the Cathedral of Christ the Saviour and the old town. "We need to focus on the middle class. And the middle class for the most part use the bank's services within the business district. We just need to shift the emphasis from the outskirts of the city to the centre."

For anyone who'd been in the Sberbank branch on Lublinskaya Street, or on Moscow's periphery at all, this attitude would have seemed strange. What about the queues, the unmet demand? But Poletaev had said only as much as he had wanted to say: the focus was shifting to where the money was. In residential districts, the vast majority of customers went to the bank exclusively to pay bills or to collect pensions and social security benefits. According to a nationwide survey conducted by the Public Opinion Foundation, more than half (51%) of those paying for communal apartments did not work. According to other studies, the proportion of pensioners and unemployed people among them was lower, but was nonetheless a significant figure — 32%. At the same time, those who exhibited demand for products more profitable to the bank, such as credit cards and mortgages, were concentrated in the centre. In 70-80% of cases, people preferred to deal with financial matters during the working week and, as a rule, near to their workplaces. Home and weekends were kept free of banking.

More rational distribution of offices became part of Poletaev's programme for turning Moscow's branch network into one of Sberbank's success stories. In this new frame of reference, Moscow was to serve as the model of working technologies and high returns. In Russia's richest city, it was a sin not to be ambitious. The capital offered a rare chance to properly satisfy a demanding public. Paying attention to customers more interested in the standard of service than its cost was what Harvard professor Anthony P. Hourihan urged management to do during the strategic seminar he delivered at the bank. And where, if not Moscow, should his advice be followed?

According to various parameters, Sberbank's Moscow business accounted for 20-25% of the bank's total. Looking at revenue alone, this figure was even higher, attested Vasily Pozdyshev, deputy chairman of the Moscow Sberbank and in charge of the bank's finances in the capital (he later went on to work for the Central Bank). Management reasoned that if a quarter of the bank could be reformed successfully in Moscow, then rolling these reforms out to the rest of the country was a mere technicality. Neither an individual lean lab, nor even the entire network, would by themselves serve as a convincing illustration of Gref and his team's vision. Moscow itself was evidence of what one senior manager rather pretentiously described to me as "the potential for mental rebirth". The capital was destined to become the place where the transformations that had occurred first took shape as a mass consumer experience.

The ten-year interval between crises was enough for Moscow to improve its financial state. From 2000 to 2007 inclusive, the Russian capital's income increased almost five and a half times, to 956 billion roubles. Officials in Moscow were overjoyed: "The city's budget is second only to that of New York", announced Mayor Luzhkov proudly in autumn 2007. At least a third of the city's treasury revenue was provided by the income of Muscovites, who at that point accounted for 20% of the total income of all Russians. The waiting list for popular car makes was months long. At weekends, shopping malls in the capital resembled rush hour on the metro. Overnight, the already golden square metres of largely wretched Moscow real estate became platinum-clad. Over the course of 2006 alone, analysts at industry portal irn.ru recorded an 88% rise in the price of urban housing, growing from $2,232 to $4,193 per square metre. Moscow's status as one of the most expensive cities on the planet came as no surprise — it was taken as a given.

Did Sberbank get its own piece of the pie? Frenzied expansion of consumer lending in Moscow had, over the years, largely passed it by. According to data produced by marketing agency Mediaplan, in 2006, Sberbank's share of the Moscow private lending market amounted to 17.9%, and subsequently fell further. Sberbank's attempts to claw back its position with specialised express lending were unsuccessful. The experiment, titled 'Quick Money', was a belated response to the successes of Russian Standard, and was considered a failure by management due to the unusually high level of arrears it generated.

> Sberbank employs around 1% of the working female population of Russia. In the Moscow Sberbank, women make up 80% of the workforce.
>
> Sberbank data.

Sberbank's attempts to take advantage of the capital's new-found wealth were hindered by its own local management system. The 13 main branches active in the city were directly operated by one head office. Even first-year management students understood that it was undesirable to have any more than seven to ten subjects under a single direct control; 13 was possible, but far from ideal. At Sberbank, the basic principles of management were being subverted. In another instance, according to branch department director Natalya Gribkova, the North-West adminstration of the bank ran five major branches. Branches in St Petersburg and Leningradskaya Oblast lower in the hierarchy were also subordinated to the same administration.

The head of the retail division would set tasks and monitor how they were progressing with the assistance of his 26 subordinates (the tasks themselves and the parameters used to measure their success varied: market share percentages for large branches, and number of products sold for the smaller ones). In Moscow, the situation was exacerbated by the fact that each of this devil's dozen of branches could, in terms of the scale of its business, easily compete with the next ten regional Sberbanks, leading to an excess of self-importance with none of the discipline. In essence, Sberbank in Moscow had 13 separate relationships with the local authorities, 13 separate sets of service standards and 13 separate staffing, lending and tariff policies. According to Pozdyshev, it all came down to a price war, with major corporate clients able to induce competition between these banking fiefdoms. Andrei Kazmin had been immensely proud of the scheme he'd devised; in a farewell interview, when his move to Russian Post was already sealed, he listed it among his ten greatest achievements at the bank.

CHAPTER 15 • AN UNLUCKY NUMBER

However, there had been a specific background to why such a system had been implemented in Moscow. Since 1986, the Moscow Sberbank had been run by Gennady Soldatenkov. Older hands spoke of how Soldatenkov and the capricious Alla Aleshkina, both Sberbank deputy chiefs, had enjoyed an uneasy relationship. Soldatenkov was marked out by his independent thinking, and in Kazmin's team, where loyalty was valued above all else, he was not a comfortable fit. Immediately after Yashin's resignation, Soldatenkov (who was one of those who did not want to see an outsider in charge of the bank) recommended senior vice-president Anatoly Barabash's candidacy to the Central Bank. It was rumoured that Soldatenkov — the last of Yashin's team — was tolerated in the new board thanks only to the protection the Moscow Sberbank boss enjoyed from Mayor Yuri Luzhkov. When Aleshkina was promoted to first deputy chairman, tensions only increased, and his relationship with the bank's president immediately worsened; Soldatenkov's former assistants recalled their boss being held in a meeting with Kazmin for several hours. The situation came to a head in 2000. During an organisational shake-up, the Moscow Sberbank administration was dissolved, and along with it, Soldatenkov's job. The deputy chairman was offered a position overseeing a number of operational departments, such as cash transactions and logistics. There were at least two dozen such sub-departments in the bank: in the silent language of head office, this meant only one thing: just leave! Soldatenkov left the bank in January 2001, becoming deputy chairman at VTB, then known as Vneshtorgbank (and later went on to become one of the heads at the Bank of Moscow).

Moscow Sberbank's revival came about under the auspices of a centralisation drive. All back-office and support functions were moved upstairs, helping to bring to self-sustaining levels the voracious appetites of the branches, whose numbers had been reduced to 12, while tightening their managers' belts. The good old days were over: "Imagine I'm a branch manager and I've had my chief accountant and administration head taken off me", said Poletaev with mock concern. "Who will I call to have my car washed? And they've taken my driver, one of the three: two to drive me around, and the third for my family. Our actions naturally caused consternation."

The rank and file felt the changes no less acutely. Poletaev acknowledged the Muscovites' dissatisfaction, but felt it understandable. On top of the huge reorganisation it had already undergone, the capital was subjected to constant experimentation. The other regional banks were learning to swim with arm-bands while a lifeguard looked on, but not in Moscow. It was there that the first SSCs had appeared, where the first credit factory had gone operational, and the site of one of the first lean labs. It was also where the most desperate attempts to refocus branch personnel on selling bank products had been made: in the capital, there were people who could actually afford them.

The wealthy client was a trophy the commercial banks had won and Sberbank had lost in the early 1990s. Their neglect of service standards over so many years had not been without consequence: Moscow's new millionaire set avoided Sberbank like the plague. But now the bank was ready to restore what it saw as the natural order of things. The decision was made to focus on the most profitable depositors from the client base, automatically putting Sberbank among the national leaders in terms of funds generated by a privileged clientèle, predominantly Muscovites. Special service zones given over to the "mass affluent segment" began to appear in branches. Those seeking to make a deposit of 8 million rubles or more (in Moscow, at least; the limit was around half that in the provinces) could bypass the queue and the stock responses of a gloomy clerk ensconced behind tinted glass, and instead have the matter dealt with in the more tranquil surrounds of the manager's office over a cup of coffee. On Novy Arbat, one of Moscow's most famous city centre streets, Sberbank opened a VIP office. The décor befitted a plush business centre and was as removed from an average branch as a deluxe hotel suite is from a mountainside bothy. Sberbank even began to give consideration to multifamily offices — specialised centres serving the financial interests of a few wealthy families. Alexei Chernikov, once involved in the development of the "A-club" network (Alpha Bank's elite service centres), assured me that Sberbank's entry into this niche market would happen sooner than expected. Forbes magazine repeatedly found more billionaires in the Russian capital than in any other city in the world, so why wasn't Sberbank viewing them as potential customers?

With rare exception, the oppressive atmosphere of the Moscow branches displayed few of the amenities those with fat wallets were accustomed to. The bank had still to get its retail business in order and teach its staff the basics of sales. Training sessions generously laid on by the company provided some assistance, but couldn't promise miracles: "For employees on the ground, in the branches, offering the customer something new? Heaven forbid. They're just asking for another queue", retail lending head Natalya Karaseva observed. Moreover, customers had strong suspicions

"Greatness lies not in being strong, but in knowing how to use that strength. Inattention to staff, and rudeness and negligence on the part of managers must be eliminated."

Letter from German Gref to staff.

about what they were being sold. The vast majority understood any piece of plastic that had the bank logo on it to be a credit card. When customers were offered credit cards in addition to their existing debit cards, they simply turned them down. Deputy chairman for retail Alexander Torbakhov calculated the likelihood of "I don't need it" or "I already have one" in reply to such an offer at 90%. It always befell staff to explain patiently which was which.

Poletaev paid no heed to such difficulties. Moscow's unrealised commercial potential was driving him mad. "Today, we're selling worse than Russia, two and a half times worse. But by this quarter we'll start selling better than Russia. In two years time, we'll be selling two and a half times better than Russia", were his rousing words.

Olga Balashova, head of training and development at the Moscow Sberbank, recalls the sales campaign with horror. "The train was already on its way and we'd only just bolted the wheels on", she said. "There was neither a system in place, nor even hands-on control — it was just shooting in the dark." Poletaev's boundless energy and the perseverance of his managers carried it through. But this alone did not explain the terrifying pace of things.

Managers were beginning to feel the pressure growing from on high. Gref believed that Moscow should set the example for the rest of the country. He demanded a breakthrough, fearing that enthusiasm for change was fast running out. After two years of reform, many people felt as if all the juice had been squeezed out of them. Gref had known in advance that the first period would be very tough, but couldn't have known that what awaited would exceed his worst expectations. The bank, rushing towards change, ran headlong into the financial crisis.

CHAPTER 16
"OUT OF THE BLUE"

REFORM DOESN'T HAPPEN IN A VACUUM. THE MARKET binds its participants in the most intricate ties. When provincial US banks started granting so-called subprime mortgages to those without secure earnings, Wall Street issued high-yield bonds backed by this kind of credit, and international funds sunk billions in securities, they were all playing with a fire that flared up around the world, including in Russia.

In the West, the fun had already begun by the start of 2008. Lehman Brothers, one of the world's leading investment banks, with a 150-year history and assets worth $639 billion, was balanced on a precipice over which it was dragged in autumn of that year by the weight of its accumulated debts. Bankruptcy threatened entire nations. Iceland's government saw the dark clouds on the horizon, but there was little it could do to stop their advance. The external liabilities of its four largest banks alone exceeded the country's GDP more than seven times over. But in Russia, hope remained that this nightmare could be avoided. Officials were initially reluctant to bandy the word 'crisis' around publicly. Finance minister Alexei Kudrin described Russia as "an island of stability" in a global ocean of liquidity problems. That quintessentially Russian appeal to blind faith was heard loudest.

Alas, the peace was short-lived. The stuttering visible on the Russian stock market in May had turned into a headlong collapse by the end of the summer.

> "The worse thing that could happen would be for oil prices to fall. If the country as a whole is finding it hard, then we'll have problems."
>
> Interview with German Gref, *Vedomosti* (11.11.2011).

Oil prices, the shaky foundation upon which the nation's wealth was built, began to drop. Significant capital drain, falling investment ratings for Russia's largest banks, some of whom were by September no longer able to meet their obligations, and finally the devaluation of the rouble — the bad news grew like a rolling snowball.

"It's awful when a situation appears out of the blue", Gref said later of that calamitous autumn. Sberbank's external borrowings did not exceed 5%, so its immediate situation was not quite so serious. Nonetheless, trouble was not long in rearing its head. Russia's biggest creditor faced the threat of defaults on corporate debt, and this was a truly huge amount. Over 40% of corporate loans issued in Russia were owed to Sberbank: a cool 3.6 trillion roubles, or slightly under 9% of GDP.

Those who had predicted the failure of Gref's project and had regarded his appointment over an experienced financier such as Kazmin a mistake now looked set to be proven right. Everything was moving along nicely in that regard: the global crisis promised to be protracted and, in all likelihood, the most serious since the Great Depression. The bank could not afford to maintain the momentum of change while all this was going on around them. It was one thing to be a reformer in a growing market, quite another in a collapsing one.

And lo! The moment of truth! The well-wishers rubbed their hands: as the crisis deepened, Gref's dreams of breathing new life into Sberbank were dissolving quicker than April snow. Of course, what was happening was not a matter of life or death. The US government, in deciding to bail out Citibank and Bank of America, had reason to wonder whether it wasn't better simply to leave them to wallow in a cesspit of their own making. Russia's largest bank, more than half of which belonged to the state, would not be the subject of such soul-searching. No one wanted to start a riot among depositors, least of all the authorities. Sberbank was still paying compensation to those whose savings had been wiped out by the hyperinflation of 1991. In 1998, history had, in part, repeated itself. Calls by finance officials to transfer savings from at-risk banks to Sberbank backfired to the degree that citizens who had believed state warnings found themselves unable to withdraw their money for several months. When they did eventually withdraw it, they discovered huge losses due to the exchange rate disparities. Would the state deceive its citizens for a third time? Such a scenario was difficult to imagine. On the other hand, who could have any real idea what awaited Russia?

Deputy chairman Stanislav Kuznetsov claimed that in April 2008, Gref and his analysts had reasonably accurately predicted the crisis worsening in the autumn. For them, talk of Russia's ability to absorb the shock was complacent nonsense. Gref had been preparing for a "hot autumn", but couldn't fully have anticipated the severity of the blow landed on the Russian economy.

By May, the bank had rid itself of risky securities worth billions. Planes from the US flew to Russia laden with bundles of dollars, the panic having induced them to order more than usual. Extra banknote cassettes were purchased to ensure the smooth functioning of ATMs. The bank made it through the most difficult autumn and winter months, as customers had no difficulty withdrawing cash. For all the nervousness on the financial markets, the

"Problems in the banking sector and problems at Sberbank are slightly different at the moment, because we won't have any issues with capitalisation this year."

Interview with German Gref on *Pozner*. (15.06.2009).

population's continued access to its money markedly relieved the tension — no one wanted a repeat of 1998. But ahead, an impenetrable fog lay heavy on the horizon. Would the economy continue to spiral downwards, or recover quickly from the shock?

"We need to be ready for a three-year crisis", Gref prophesied at a meeting with journalists in early February 2009. This was a bad forecast for the bank. Internal restructuring was sidelined, although Gref himself would never admit this: "Yes, it's a very difficult time", he wrote to colleagues, "but above all we make it difficult for ourselves when we start to flounder and deviate from the path we've chosen for ourselves." Working in a tumbling economy with no clear prospects for recovery created anxieties. To be on the safe side, Sberbank borrowed 0.5 trillion roubles from the Central Bank (a subordinated loan that exceeded what the other banks combined received from the state) — while the demand for money had not been so acute, the bank's capital adequacy was above the norm.

In estimating a three-year crisis, Gref had been overly pessimistic. But when the economic problems were at their height, such sentiments seemed natural. Over the course of the first six months of 2009 alone, the share of non-performing loans (in arrears by more than 90 days) in the bank's portfolio tripled. The bank rewrote its business plan, abandoning the previous pace of increased lending. Lending terms for every category of client became much stricter. Sberbank didn't see anything encouraging on the horizon, and some of its representatives made no bones about this fact.

Alexei Chuvin, Sberbank's director of construction lending, stated publicly that the credit-guzzling building market stood at the edge of an abyss. The

> "I was called in the middle of the night and told I had no right to speak on behalf of Sberbank. This despite my frequent participation in conferences, some international, where I'd never once had to have my presentations or addresses approved."
>
> Interview with Alexei Chuvin, Forbes. (26.08.2009).

CHAPTER 16 · "OUT OF THE BLUE"

pronouncement had been made at an industry conference, where delegates had expected to hear a reassuring report about how the crisis had been overcome. They were up off their seats almost as soon as he opened his mouth. Chuvin primarily predicted a collapse in square metre values. Banks were experiencing higher rates of arrears, and with this a growing volume of real estate collateral on their balance sheets. "Banks are beginning to shed real estate, as property owners themselves are doing. I think this will create an additional wave that will sweep the market. Along with the crises in banking, one wave may overlap the next, and I think the situation will become very serious", warned the expert.

Such developments did not bode well for Sberbank. Chuvin himself had been part of a lending policy that had seen developers granted 600 billion roubles in loans — 15% of the total portfolio. His frankness infuriated the bank's management, and they let him know this in no uncertain terms. Gref himself had stern words with Chuvin, and when he continued to defend his position, this was strike one against his name. Strike two was his decision to decorate his speech with macroeconomic arguments, despite not being versed in the subject. Rashly spilling confidential information related to one particular deal was strike three. Finally, he simply had no right to speak on behalf of the bank, since he was on leave pending dismissal at the time.

The bank insisted that the manager's departure was unrelated to his unauthorised statements. "We would have reprimanded him for that, not fired him", stated Gref publicly. Chuvin's dismissal created a stir, and he was painted as a martyr for the truth, although it was more likely he'd simply exceeded his authority. After all, the bank had not denied the problem he'd outlined — property development was in a coma, and developers were not expected to recover from their financial predicament quickly. By September, it became clear that Sberbank was facing an avalanche of bankruptcies as soon as the crisis got into full swing. It was clear the bank did not know how to deal with desperate debtors, and its lack of preparedness for such an eventuality meant the bank had neither adequate mechanisms nor the expertise to claw its money back. The last time it had made any steps in this regard was back in 1998, and over the intervening ten years, the gears of those mechanisms had rusted over, while Sberbank had never had much of a reputation on the market for zealously pursuing debt in any case. Resolving complex financial and legal conflicts had traditionally been left to its security department, which was a little like leaving a bomb disposal team in charge of a nuclear reactor.

In 1992, MAIR Industrial Group founder Viktor Makushin sealed his first major deal: selling 14 wagons' worth of scrap metal to a man with a plan for it. By the time I met Makushin 11 years later, it took him some time to list all the companies that made up his diverse group. "More than 50, maybe 56, including Ukraine," the businessman told me, peering over a long list. "We're always buying something, selling something; I can't keep track of it all."

By the start of the 2000s, as well as his metal business, Makushin was investing in new sectors, from the forestry and and paint industries to engineering and microbiology. MAIR's impressively large advertising boards were visible on the walls of the Kremlin itself. The group's offices were, however, hidden away behind the dull concrete of a block on the outskirts of the

CHAPTER 16 • "OUT OF THE BLUE"

city. It was more reminiscent of a secure facility than a business centre, fitting for a man who'd made his fortune during the lawless 1990s.

Makushin's empire had seemed indestructible, but the crisis paid no heed to such reputations. The 2.25 billion roubles that MAIR had borrowed from Sberbank to carry out technical refits at its plants proved to be fatal. The numbers no longer added up.

The company was suspected of having no intention of repaying the debt, and criminal proceedings were launched in relation to fraud and intentional bankruptcies among companies belonging to the group. The 'About the Company' section on MAIR's official website still informs the reader that by the middle of 2008, the group's financial position was still stable, despite the enormous debt burden, but was then "attacked by authorities of the Russian Federation, as a result of which [the group] was deprived of a large part of its assets".

This was a fugitive debtor's version of events. In the midst of this debt conflict, Makushin chose not to participate personally in its resolution, and instead left the country.

The bank took a philosophical view of it all: everyone reacts to stress differently. One can spend 15 years building a company and live like a billionaire, but when things fall to pieces, people are faced with a tough choice. One possible response is to work like hell for five years or so, not in order to amass a fortune, but to repay the debt. But those approaching their fifties and sixties found it harder than others. Working days on end, they'd missed their children growing up, and now they were expected to go through it all again. Some borrowers threw their hands up and told the bankers that they just didn't have the energy.

"It's obvious that during a crisis it's no longer possible to seriously restructure the economy of a major bank."

Interview with German Gref, *Vedomosti*. (26.09.2008)

The other way is more appealing that the first: to jet off to warmer climes, picking off the juicer parts of the business beforehand and leaving their creditors the bones to gnaw on. This could be done with a cunning bit of manoeuvring that wrong-footed the clumsy state bank: it was used to dealing with money, not rolling mills and oil fields. The plan only had one major drawback: the bank was now under new management, and this one meticulously accounted for every penny. Fooling such a creditor was now not only much harder; it was also dangerous.

CHAPTER 17
KICKING CLIENTS WHEN THEY'RE DOWN?

"IF YOU WERE TO ASK ME WHAT THE CRISIS HAS taught us, my answer would be: how to recover debts", Sberbank finance director Anton Karamzin told me. From this point on, he had no doubt that whatever happened on the markets, the bank would be able to cope. Karamzin held 80% of his personal savings in Sberbank shares. The other 20% was in 'hard' cash, again held in deposit accounts at the bank. In 2011, Karamzin bought additional shares in Sberbank, worth 23.4 million roubles, on the market. Already the largest shareholder on the board, he had boosted his stake to 0.003%, more than four times larger than Gref's (0.0007%). "I believe in the long-term growth of the company. What will that be?" Karamzin simply shrugged.

Our conversation, over a mug of invigorating green tea, came at a time when world markets were again in a state of fever. Europe's debt problems were intensified by the worrying situation in the US, which had just had its credit rating downgraded for the first time in its history. Oil prices were plummeting, followed closely by Russian stock indices, a situation that did not bode well for the future. But Karamzin was not inclined to over-dramatise events. Compared to 2008's tsunami, these seemed like a few nervous ripples.

The crisis required Sberbank to turn its focus towards protecting its own interests. The economy was growing weaker every day. The collapse threatened not only individual companies but whole industries. Firstly, the bank set up a department for working with bad assets (DWBA). Problem debtors needed to know that they were up against some tough negotiators — constructive and willing to compromise, but ruthless in the face of any deceit. The DWBA team originally comprised six members, but they could handle only a small fraction of the work that was required. One department manager in the middle of it all recalled how working days would roll on until two or three in the morning. Nonetheless, this did not make much of a dent in the catalogue of problems requiring urgent action from the bank. In a matter of months, there were ten times as many people working in the department than when it was launched.

So as not to overcomplicate lines of communication, DWBA director Svetlana Sagaidak worked directly under Gref. Problem debt owed by major clients is a particularly delicate subject for any bank, and it wasn't desirable to have too many in the know. Sagaidak also headed up the board of directors at sister company Sberbank Capital, which managed non-core assets. As a result, she was able to control the entire cycle of operations for debt recovery, from the initial negotiations for debt restructuring to the sale of property or businesses acquired by the bank in lieu of payment. Colleagues considered Sagaidak a difficult person to please. Managers at the bank would put hours into convincing her that a certain borrower was no major source of concern, only for her to emerge even less assured.

Before the crisis, the country had been in the grip of a retail frenzy. Grocery retail exhibited insane levels of growth, and entrepreneurs jumping on the grocery bandwagon believed that it was in fact a gravy train. Alexei Podsokhin, one of the founders and former president of the Siberian hypermarket chain Alli, was named Ernst & Young's international Entrepreneur of the Year for 2007. After shops and poultry plants, the businessman planned to throw up skyscrapers in Siberia's cities. In 2007, Oleg Bolychev, founder of the modest Kaliningrad-based retailer Vester, promised to increase his supermarket revenue 12 times in 18 months to $2.2 billion. In the same pre-crisis year, former CEO of retail chain Mosmart Eric Blondeau was confidently giving estimates for the construction of a federation-wide, multiformat chain to compete with French-owned Auchan. Such development was made possible mainly by borrowing. By 2009, almost a quarter of Sberbank's credit portfolio was tied up in the retail trade. All these companies soon found themselves forced to reassess their plans for aggressive expansion. With the onset of the crisis, all bets were off — the only thing guaranteed was backbreaking debt.

"In this life, everything can go wrong at any point. That's why I'm deliberately sceptical of good news. I think it's better to be safe than sorry", explained Sagaidak. Her scepticism manifested itself on the credit committees covering the "yellow zone" — according to internal classification, those clients with a satisfactory plan for debt servicing: How long would that plan hold up? What about guarantees? What were their market prospects like? Many remembered Sberbank as a lackadaisical and forgiving lender, but this image was now very much a thing of the past. The bank wanted to know about any problems its borrowers might be having as soon as they appeared.

> "In order for us not to be forced to impose severe administrative measures, each of us must work under our own initiative to actively reduce costs."
>
> Letter from German Gref to employees, (01.09.2008).

Of course, Sberbank wasn't about to set the hounds on its debtors, viewing the shock-and-awe measures that Alfa Bank chose to employ with little enthusiasm. There were some real giants among Alfa's borrowers, primarily Rusal, Russia's largest producer of aluminium, the global price of which had collapsed at the outset of the crisis. The bank methodically sought bankruptcy for the companies of the group owned by oligarch Oleg Deripaska, and was the only one of its creditors to flatly refuse debt restructuring. It believed that legal action and court judgements was a more efficient way of getting the bank's money back than any attempts at empathy towards or understanding of its debtor's position. "Kicking our clients when they're already down is not how we do things", Sagaidak said. As far as she was concerned, working with major borrowers required a cautious and sober assessment of the potential implications. Bankrupting a large company could start a chain reaction; problems would appear within the small and medium businesses that depended on it, and it could eventually lead to a run on the banks. The banking market was already in dire straits. Sagaidak was convinced that no system of deposit guarantees would save even the most stable bank if customers began storming its branches to get their money on the spot.

Two years on from the crisis, Sberbank counted around 1,600 cases of bankruptcy among its borrowers, more than any other credit institution in the country. I was told that in each of these cases, negotiations on restructuring the loan had come to nothing, or had been doomed from the outset. The lender was inclined to come to some agreement provided it was a last chance. Finding a way out of such debt impasses was impossible on one's own; cooperation with the bank was essential. "Sometimes it was the case that were clients given a bit more flexibility and the situation assessed a little more realistically, bankruptcy could be avoided," Sagaidak reasoned.

In one such example, Sberbank called on Alexander Fedorov, founder of nationwide lingerie chain Dikaya Orhideya (and whose controlling share was pledged to the bank, not to secure the original loan but as part of the terms of its restructuring) to be more frugal in his expenditure. The businessman had blown $3 million on the company's head office alone, and the state the company was in could not be considered a model of sanity. Fedorov's business had been on the verge of turning a profit, but the lightest tremor in the market had pushed it back into the red. For companies that had already defaulted, cost-cutting measures were as natural an instinct as breathing, but not for Fedorov. He wasn't interested in letting his creditors tell him how to run his business. The entrepreneur was sure things would pick up and bankruptcy could be avoided. His intuition failed him. In spring 2011, financial recovery procedures were instigated against the company. "God knows, we've done everything in our power not to add a business that sells bras to our collection of collateral", the bank joked, plaintively.

Sberbank hadn't the slightest desire to become a dumping ground for a ragtag assembly of assets. From meeting to meeting, Gref never tired of repeating that he had no wish for the country's biggest bank, with its neatly balanced books, turning into another financial-industrial group. Minor collateral such as transport, cheaper property, and fittings were dispensed with at the earliest opportunity. Fortunately, this proved simple enough, as much of it could be sold off at auction for a decent price, with Sberbank co-founding the St Petersburg-based Auction House of the Russian Federation. The bank was also able to shift other items via its in-house electronic trade system, Sberbank-AST. The bad debts of small enterprises (up to 500 million roubles in arrears by six months) were handed over to collection agencies. With larger debts and collateral, the situation was very different, with the bank expending enormous amounts of energy (proportional to the sums involved) in keeping it under control.

Established in August 2008 as a wholly-owned subsidiary company of the bank, Sberbank Capital was conceived as a 'special situation fund': a structure for managing non-core assets during periods of calm. Sberbank was not always the creditor; among Sberbank Capital's interests were long-term investment projects in which the bank wanted its own stake. However, with the onset of the crisis, the bank was forced to turn its ploughshares into swords. Sberbank Capital got the go ahead from its parent bank to begin laying into debtors and their assets. German Gref decided to entrust the running of the specialist company to an equally special individual.

In American writer Tom Wolfe's novel, *A Man In Full*, the reader is introduced to the colourful Harry Zale, an arrears manager and "work-out artiste" who represents the interests of PlannersBanc. Meanwhile, Atlanta's largest real estate developer, owned by the novel's main protagonist, owes the bank half a billion dollars. Tricky negotiations with this local real estate king fall on the shoulders of Zale, a former US Marine, who dons his trademark skull-and-crossbones emblazoned braces for the occasion. He proceeds to reduce the arrogant, all-powerful businessmen to what they really are — palpitating debtors squirming uncomfortably in their seats.

I am reminded of Harry Zale every time anyone describes to me Ashot Khachaturyants, head of Sberbank Capital. Colleagues treated him with reverence, and said they couldn't imagine anyone better suited to the job. One manager at Sberbank who frequently worked with Khachaturyants on projects described him as "a specialist with rare talents." He had, my source told me confidentially, contacts in high places. More importantly, however, he was extremely smart and calculating. Any attempt to outsmart him was a waste of time. He was a frequent champion of the 'Mafia' role-playing tournaments popular among Russian businessmen, demonstrating an aptitude that proved relevant to his line of work. The ability to expose the deception and cunning of one's opponents was key to the game. To succeed at 'Mafia', one had to have a sharp intellect, a keen understanding of human psychology, and an actor's guile. The man tasked by the country's biggest bank to deal with its most difficult instances of non-payment exhibited all of these characteristics in abundance.

Before Sberbank Capital, Ashot Khachaturyants had gained valuable experience in the civil service. After working in the oil industry in the 1990s, he ended up in the Ministry for Economic Development and Trade shortly after Gref had taken over. As advisor to the minister, Ashot had initially been responsible for dealings with Gazprom, before taking over the department for investment policy. This naturally granted him access to key people within the larger state companies. "The majority of large business owners have known me personally for a long time," said Khachaturyants in an interview with *Vedomosti*.

He also spent time working for the FSB, where he'd been responsible for looking after funds designated for border management in the Caucasus.

Since its inception, Sberbank Capital had been an information black hole. There was plenty of press speculation about it — more than the bank would have liked. "The size of our 'daughter' has been greatly hypertrophied by the press. Its assets don't constitute even 1% of Sberbank's total assets", was deputy chairman Andrei Donskikh's response to journalists' questioning. "This is peanuts compared to the 8 trillion roubles the total assets are valued at", echoed Karamzin. However, Khachaturyants' role in resolving debt issues continued to raise questions. Why did the bank deal with some debtors directly, while others were passed on to its subsidiary? How did this relate to the size of the debt?

In actual fact, there was no correlation. Sagaidak's department worked with loans that could still be repaid. But when a company was unable to repay the debt in cash, depending on the collateral agreement, the debtor's property or business was transferred to the creditor. Metallurgical and automobile plants, supermarket chains, grain companies and elite residential complexes — it made no sense for the bank to keep them on its balance sheet. It willingly passed this Noah's Ark on to Sberbank Capital, whose task was now to jettison such ballast as profitably as possible.

Anton Karamzin, Svetlana Sagaidak and Vadim Kulik, the bank's chief risk assessor, travelled to Europe in early 2009 to see how 'distressed assets' were dealt with there. They spent a number of days at companies such as Archon Group, one of the world's largest asset management companies (and part of

---

"People often talk about the benefits of state banks. One of our main benefits is the free provision of a large number of services."

Interview with German Gref, *RIA Novosti*. (23.04.2010).

Goldman Sachs' empire). "We had to be on the inside to get a proper chance to study how it all worked," recalled Karamzin. Western banks, as a rule, preferred to leave it up to subsidiary companies to rake the Augean stables clean of the remnants of the global recession. Lending institutions were not ideally suited to completing unfinished apartment blocks or carrying out offshore exploration when the final aim was to sell it all off. Moreover, the average bank bureaucracy, with its convoluted system of approval and complex regulatory framework, was not particularly attuned to making quick decisions when these were exactly what was required. Sagaidak expressed the same idea rather more succinctly: "If something's on fire, don't go around collecting signatures. Put it out!"

Sberbank Capital was as removed from the DWBA as an anti-terror unit is from the Court of Arbitration. As one insider at the bank explained, their shared goal was to ensure loans were repaid, but their methods and the operating freedoms afforded to each were very different. Everything needed to be kept under strict control. At any moment, the bank's position on the list of creditors could be undermined and its assets pillaged. If the palace guard is not rotated, there'll soon be nothing in the palace to guard. Sberbank Capital acted decisively, unceremoniously dealing with those who looked like they were about to 'do a runner'.

Online media outlets tripped over each other to publish incriminating information about the company's activities. A Google search of the subsidiary would bring up stories about "Sberbank Capital's most recent hostile takeover" as the first entry after the official website. In spring 2011, the investigative eye of weekly publication The New Times, renowned for its bold exposés of government corruption, turned on Khachaturyants. The magazine was run by the rather eccentric Yevgenia Albats, grande dame of the free Russian press, whose doctorate from Harvard did not temper scathing judgements of her fellow journalists. The magazine published an article titled "Hostile takeover: how the state picked apart privately-owned Energomash", which asserted that Alexander Stepanov, the industrial holding company's founder and under arrest for fraud at the time, was a victim of the brutal policies of Sberbank, which was acting in the interests of those close to the government.

The scandalous article did not elicit an immediate response from Sberbank's PR department. The bank clearly did not wish to discredit itself by giving credence to accusations that were so patently ridiculous. Independent director Sergei Guriev decided to throw his hat in the ring regardless. The inaccuracies of The New Times' diatribe had hit a raw nerve for him. Relationships between the bank and the press were not part of the supervisory board's remit — this was what the Public Relations Department was for — but Guriev feared that the bank's reputation would suffer if it left the charges unanswered.

Guriev suspected that Alexander Stepanov was not the picture of innocence he'd been painted to be. His reputation on the financial market was already widely known. Stepanov had not repaid a large loan from the Kazakh bank BTA, leading to legal action that went all the way to the High Court in London. As a result of the defendant's continual no-shows at hearings, he was sentenced in absentia to two years in Pentonville Prison for contempt of court (the same prison that had once briefly held the writer Oscar Wilde, albeit on very different charges). In the Sberbank case, it was difficult to see Stepanov as the righteous martyr journalists had portrayed the Energomash owner to be. Guriev began to go through what he knew of the case. Had Sberbank really been the one that had bankrupted Energomash's main companies, or had it been the companies themselves? When was this supposed to have happened? In 2008, after Energomash, who'd received a loan from Sberbank worth more than 17 billion roubles, had stopped repaying it. The outstanding debt exceeded 12 billion roubles — more than enough to tempt Energomash to cut and run. Sberbank appealed to the Prosecutor General, and Stepanov ended up behind bars. The eventual reason for his conviction wasn't Energomash's bankruptcy as such, but the asset stripping that was occurring right under the bank's nose. But who was likely to see it that way? From the outside, it all seemed clear enough: the monstrous state bank cynically pursuing a prey that had had the imprudence to take on debt just before the crisis hit. In the public's consciousness, the influence the bank enjoyed undermined any justifications for the legality of its actions. The entrepreneur couldn't pay off his debts and went to jail — it seemed cut and dried. Property seizure? Wasn't that just the usual way to settle accounts in Russia when such powerful players were calling the shots? Asserting a different version of events and you were playing to a tough crowd.

Guriev decided not to limit himself to a general discussion on the rights of lenders, but to explain the deliberate malice behind what had gone on. He carefully went through all the materials related to the case and wrote a detailed response to The New Times.

The scheme, common in Russian business, that Guriev outlined in his letter looked like this: Company

A owes half a billion dollars to Bank B; the company knows it is unable to repay the debt, so bankruptcy will inevitably follow and all its assets transferred to the bank's ownership. How does a shareholder in Company A ensure that at least some of the assets remain in his hands? He must make it appear that A has a liability (for $0.5 billion or even more) to offshore Company C, the ultimate beneficiary of which is this shareholder in A. Then, provided the representatives of Company C are on the ball, it will obtain a substantial portion of the assets of Company A to the detriment of the honest Johns at Bank B. But how is such a liability created? This requires another offshore, Company D. Company C presents a Russian court with an agreement which states that, a long time ago, offshore Company C lent $0.5 billion to Company D, with Company A serving as a guarantee, as well as evidence that D has not repaid in accordance with the agreement, so now C is entitled to recover this debt in the form of Company A.

"Some people think: look at that greedy shark with money to burn," mused Karamzin. "You think, what's a couple of hundred million dollars to them? But this monster is made up of old men's kopecks. The entire banking system is oriented towards the middle classes, and it's only us who will deal with pensioners. You rob grandmothers and do a runner? We'll catch you, you can be sure of that. We won't take any more than our due, but we'll get what's ours."

By late spring 2009, it was clear the bank was beginning to claw its way out of the debt hole it had been stuck in. Time and again, the prognoses pointed to a downturn in the economy, but those waiting expectantly for good news heard a note of cautious optimism in the words of World Bank experts who believed that Russia could get through the second half of the year with smaller losses than the first, and then experience moderate growth. The worst of the crisis was behind them. The problems that could have buried, if not Sberbank itself, then its ambitions for a rapid transformation, no longer seemed as ominous. The crisis and the bank's success in overcoming it had instead strengthened management's resolve to implement reforms. Increased self-confidence, a sense of relief — there was something in the air when Gref got caught up in the most astounding deal in the recent history of Russian business.

"...people are at the heart of the bank's business - their dreams and aspirations, their problems, the circumstances of their lives."

Excerpt from the anniversary publication "Sberbank: 170 years of successful development." (2011).

CHAPTER 18
MORE THAN A BANK

THE IDEA TO BUY OPEL WASN'T SBERBANK'S. IT HAD come from the management of Canadian group Magna International, one of the world's leading automotive component manufacturers. Magna's management had got to know Sberbank's president during his time in government. Shortly before Gref left the ministry, the Canadians had signed an agreement on establishing manufacturing capacity in Russia, a country in which the company had enjoyed fairly limited success. To facilitate the partnership, in 2007 Magna allowed Gorky Automobile Plant (GAZ) owner Oleg Deripaska to buy 20% of its shares. However, this share block, bought for $1.5 billion, soon ended up in the hands of the oligarch's creditors when a joint project between the Canadians and AvtoVAZ to locate an assembly plant in Togliatti and build the Lada C-class ended in ignominious fashion. State corporation Russian Technologies, which owned the Volga auto plant, eventually froze the project in its third year.

Magna's new 'Russian plan' represented something special. The company planned to throw a huge amount of money and effort behind securing a rare chance to get its hands on a legendary car brand at a decent price. They had a fight on their hands with General Motors' European business to seal the deal. The US manufacturer owned a number of Opel plants in Germany, Belgium and Spain, as well as running Vauxhall's plant in the UK.

CHAPTER 18 · MORE THAN A BANK

Attempting to buy up one of the West's most venerable car marques was a bold move. In 2009, the German manufacturer, with an almost 150 year history, marked 110 years since the first car rolled out of its plant. General Motors had acquired the company during the Great Depression: at that time, Opel was the largest car manufacturer in Germany, and the second largest in Europe. 80 years later, another global financial crisis left the Americans with a dilemma: could they really afford to keep running a business in Europe? Compared to the agonies suffered by the US automotive industry, at that time begging the government for billions of dollars in bailouts, things with Opel didn't seem so bad. "Opel is solvent — the crisis is at General Motors", affirmed the chairman of the Opel works council, Klaus Franz. Nonetheless, the Europeans were losing money at an appreciable rate. To cover 'worst-case scenario' losses, the company needed to borrow up to €1.8 billion, and a corresponding state guarantee was requested from the German government. In less fraught times, the amount would probably not have caused much of an upset, but the crisis cast an enormous shadow over a global car market that was already haemorrhaging customers. Problems with overproduction escalated rapidly. Restructuring plans (with the almost inevitable loss of tens of thousands of jobs) would not even be countenanced by the unions. Selling up was now the only option.

The purchase of Opel promised to turn Sberbank into the saviours of the national automobile industry. If the deal worked out, an entire conglomerate could be formed by rolling together Opel's core plants and at least one major Russian site. Gref believed that this Eurasian giant would be producing six million cars per year in the space of five years. It was easy enough to judge how brave such forecasts were simply by considering GM's sales in Europe in 2007, the most in the company's history: it had sold 2.2 million cars, half the number Sberbank intended to shift. No-one seemed concerned about Opel strengthening its position within the Russian market. After all, there would be local factories working for the famous German brand. Who was going to baulk at increased orders, improved use of capacity and job creation? GAZ was a more than suitable industry partner, and given Magna's connection to Deripaska it made sense. Other options were also considered. Almost every major car manufacturer in the country borrowed from Sberbank. "By and large, it was all the same to us," said Anton Karamzin. "Whoever ends up being our working partner will make great strides in development and prosperity as a result of this deal. The same applies to us — more business, larger profits, and a better standard of loan portfolio."

> "We are a large, old-fashioned bank... But we know how to make money. I don't know another institution like us."
>
> Interview with German Gref, Wall Street Journal (15.04.2011).

Gref and his team came round to the notion only after the fires of the crisis had been localised, but seized on the idea eagerly. What about it was so attractive to them? At that time, the bank was making its first tentative steps on the road to reform and was only coming to appreciate all the difficulties this new way of life threw up. The rumblings of reform boomed loudly in larger cities, but weren't reverberating to every dim and distant corner of the empire. Thousands of branches continued to plod along as if nothing had happened, and at a national level this presented an immense front for the generals of head office to contend with. For Gref, though, this presented no challenge. He knew he was in control of the situation and could have no complaints that he wasn't free to do as felt necessary. Orchestrating unheard-of numbers of redundancies, while changing everything from the behaviour, working habits and productivity to the very expressions on the faces of a workforce larger than that of Coca-Cola, IKEA, Procter & Gamble, Sony and many other transnational giants... Who else in Russia could even consider such things? Money was no object. Despite the crisis, the bank still possessed levels of capital that had the rest of the market salivating. Its net profit in 2009 had fallen by two-thirds to 36.2 billion roubles, but only because it had boosted its reserves to offset any potential losses from lending. Why not take a chance on Opel?

The deal, and the preparations leading up to it, brought Sberbank worldwide publicity. I personally know of people who, of all the financial institutions in the world, have only heard of Sberbank. But in the West, Sberbank was not considered one of the big players in the financial world (and three years after the events described, trade journal *The Banker*, whose authoritative list ranked world credit institutions by fixed capital, did not feature the bank in its top 100). Gref was convinced that the bank would inevitably work its way up the table: Sberbank planned to be one of the top ten largest banks in the world. The international media became obsessed with what the Russians were up to. "Over a few months, we were one of the most referenced companies in the world," Sberbank's boss recalled. It was considered a matter of time before shares in the bank would be offered on the global exchanges (as depositary receipts), an event that was guaranteed to attract even more of a furore. When I met Karamzin, who was never short of a joke or two, he tilted his head back and rolled his eyes comically to mimic the surprise of investors at Sberbank's presentation in New York two years later, just after they'd been told that Sberbank was the world's biggest bank.

The financiers had exchanged incredulous glances. Was this some kind of joke? But for market capitalisation, the Russian bank could count itself as the world's largest in terms of its stature in the domestic economy — this in a country that itself was not economically inconsequential (ranked sixth on GDP based on the purchasing power parity of its national currency, according to the World Bank). The GM deal would go a long way to showing that Russia's biggest bank was far from a bit-part player on the global market.

However, the biggest excitement was reserved for something else altogether. Thanks to Sberbank, Russia finally had the chance to ditch its well-deserved reputation for building some of the world's worst cars. Austrian Siegfried Wolf, at that time head of Magna, told Gref he estimated that local production standards lagged behind the world market by a minimum of three generations — around 15 years. There was no point in trying to catch up with their Western competitors 'under their own steam'. The technological gap was almost insurmountable, and the price of entry to this exclusive club was terrifyingly high. Volkswagen's management told Sberbank's boss that the outlay on a platform for the new Golf alone came to $2.5 billion, although the German manufacturer perhaps wasn't the most representative example — no-one else in the global auto industry invested so much money on engineering research. In 2010, for example, the company spent more than $9.5 billion on new development projects — three times more than GM. But even the stingiest Western

CHAPTER 18 · MORE THAN A BANK

companies seemed like outrageous spendthrifts by Russian standards. AutoVAZ's annual reports revealed their plant's outlay on such projects barely exceeded $50 million. The purchase of Opel would be a leap into the unknown.

Sberbank's tactic was to go into the deal as something between a portfolio investor and strategic investor, by completing all the financial, organisational and legal steps needed to transfer its stake in Opel to a domestic manufacturer while making a decent margin from the deal. For Sberbank, this was a whole new way of generating income. The entire deal a walk on the wild side for the bank, but it was also an exception that proved a rule, as vice-president Denis Bugrov told journalists: Sberbank still had no intention of turning into a financial-industrial group.

The peculiarity of the deal lay not so much in the motivation of the buyer as in that of the seller. Were things so bad at GM that they were forced to give up such valuable technology for a pittance? What would compel the Americans to hand over their projects to Russians (albeit in league with some Canadians), given GM's own interests in the local market? The downsides of the Russian proposal were outweighed by fear of the Chinese, the Americans' main geopolitical rival, who appeared hungry to get their hands on Western know-how; as such, Beijing Automotive's move to buy Opel was doomed from the outset.

GM was, as expected, a difficult seller. Competition among bidders, which at different times included FIAT and the Belgian investment fund RHJ International, allowed the Americans to twist the arms of the prospective buyers. Over the course of protracted negotiations, more and more obstacles sprung up in Sberbank and Magna's way. The resultant agreement

> "The satisfaction wrought from conquering a peak is the most incredible feeling - one that a person can never lose or have taken from them."
>
> Letter from German Gref to employees (09.02.2009).

was to give Sberbank a 35% stake in Opel's capital. This, combined with Magna's 20% holding, would give the partners control of the company, although not immediately. The consortium was to pay $500 million for Opel. It was expected that a fifth of the amount would go on buying up shares in the auto manufacturer, while the rest would come in the form of an interest-free loan, convertible to shares in Opel. It would be a long time — four years — before this conversion would be complete. Before then, the buyers were able to put money into the business without having full control. But the real stumbling blocks proved to be technology and patents — GM did everything in its power to resist their transfer, having invested $6.5 billion of its own money in them over the previous five years. Some time later, US diplomatic correspondence released by Wikileaks revealed that the consortium proposed 31 amendments to the text of the already signed agreement, with partners insisting on the transfer of technology, something GM apparently hadn't had in mind at the outset.

However, Sberbank regarded this expertise as central to its plans. Its vision was to create engineering and design centres where local boffins could develop engines, bodies or chassis to a modern standard at sites on the Volga. Through this, the bank envisaged the gradual emergence of a new generation of Russian engineers working at the forefront of the global automotive industry.

The invisible partners in these negotiations were governments in Washington, Brussels, Berlin and Moscow. Deals of this scale would be unthinkable without politics playing a role, and when it came to Opel, that role was a major one. In the patriotic haze that hung over the purchase, the silhouette of the

CHAPTER 18 · MORE THAN A BANK

Kremlin loomed large. It was clear that, in order to revive Russia's car industry, the state bank was picking up a baton dropped by the government as a result of its lacklustre budgetary support. Vladimir Putin rushed to call the deal one of the first steps towards "real integration with the European economy". He had already made assurances that, after the new owners took control of Opel, there would be no major lay-offs, and that management intended to work closely with the unions. The sympathies of the German government, and Angela Merkel personally, also lay with Sberbank and Magna. Despite systemic problems in the industry, primarily overcapacity, the German government did not want to hear any talk of redundancies. Not taking steps to safeguard 25,000 jobs in the lead-up to parliamentary elections planned for September was tantamount to political suicide.

Gref was torn between reforming the bank, dealing with a crisis that was still smouldering away, and the Opel deal. He was obsessed with the idea of turning the bank into a machine for realising innovative ideas, a bank for economic development. "I'm perhaps more a civil servant than a banker," Gref said of himself somewhat ironically. Despite his departure from mainstream politics, he remained keenly interested in what was going on in the political sphere. On one occasion, the bank's president gathered a group of prominent political analysts round an amber-inlaid table, the work of master craftsmen from Kaliningrad (Gref was rather proud of this particular piece). The host became so engrossed in the meeting that he ended up losing eight hours to it, throwing the rest of his schedule into disarray and leaving the minute-takers catatonic with exhaustion. Needless to say, even during a packed working week, Gref always found

"I think that what we're doing is of great importance to the development of the economy. And no less important that what the government is doing."

Interview with German Gref, *Dozhd* television station (02.02.2012).

time to speak to former colleagues in the ministry and government. He still keenly felt the failures of a state industry policy he nonetheless did his best to carry out. Simply throwing money into a resource-centred economy was not his style.

Bankrolling progress was a strategy more in keeping with the reform-minded ex-minister. To be more than just a bank was the first 'rule' in the strategy. From the very outset of his work at Sberbank, Gref had launched himself into the boldest of projects. He believed, for example, that by studying the characteristics of local markets, the bank could apply the micro-financing experiences of Nobel laureate Muhammad Yunus, founder of the renowned Grameen Bank, which provided small loans (no more than $100 on average) to poor Bangladeshi farmers. The idea did not catch on and was soon forgotten. It was quickly replaced by a crusade to make Russians more entrepreneurial. Sberbank was the first institution in Russia to finance start-ups and extend lines of credit to cafés, car washes, salons, and other small businesses.

Gref's willingness to lend a helping hand to the Russian car industry was driven by the same ideals. "We could be earning much more money from these investments," he observed during an interview with one of Russia's main TV stations. "It's quite a complex and risky purchase, unprecedented in Russian history, and one which for us is clearly not motivated by profit. It's first and foremost an attempt to help restructure our car industry."

Were the interests of the business being sacrificed? Anton Karamzin strongly rejected the suggestion. He made assurances that everything was being done on a purely commercial basis. At least the bank had no fear that the deal would be a financial disaster. Minority shareholders meanwhile tried to get their heads round what little they knew, but were left shrugging their shoulders: why was nothing being done about market capitalisation? In the space of a year, it had fallen dramatically as a result of the crisis. Why was management even getting itself involved in such a risky, time-consuming and demanding venture at all? But as Gref never tired of repeating, the main goal was importing technologies: "If that doesn't happen, we've wasted our time," he told a Sochi economic forum in September.

After six months of negotiation, Sberbank and Magna were almost in reaching distance of their goal, despite GM's continued haggling. It was now claiming for itself priority rights for reacquiring the Opel shares in the event that the new owners wanted to get rid of its stake.

The affair looked like it was drawing to a conclusion. At the end of October, GM head Fritz Henderson told The Financial Times that they were looking to complete the necessary paperwork over the coming days and close the deal by December. Gref was nervous, although he should have been used to luck deserting him in dealings with the West, having spent years fruitlessly trying to secure Russian accession to the WTO. Due to some obscure technicalities, the necessary signatures still hadn't made it onto the final documents. How long would this go on? Management had spent months in gruelling negotiations for a deal that could fall apart at the very last moment. Nonetheless, no-one saw this as a serious possibility. Defying the usual formalities, it was the press who drew a line under the long-running saga. By June, The Times was reporting, with some dismay, that "Sberbank, Vauxhall's new part-owner, is the Big Daddy of Russian

> "Judging by what we're seeing in the European press, GM didn't warn anyone about anything, didn't speak to anyone about anything, and has without prior agreement presented everyone with a fait accompli."
>
> Vladimir Putin at a meeting of the Russian government presidium (05.11.2009).

banks, practically an extension of the state budget in implementing the Kremlin's industrial policies."

However, in early November, everything fell to pieces — GM slammed the door in the buyers' faces. The market was in recovery, sales forecasts had improved, and GM had renewed faith in its own ability to dig itself out of the hole it was in. The Russians and Canadians were told in no uncertain terms that the deal was off. Berlin refused to believe what it was hearing, and an almighty row erupted.

While those involved in the deal digested the news, the Germans cursed GM's treachery. Wolfgang Porsche, chairman of the eponymous car manufacturer's supervisory board, decried the Americans' decision as a dirty trick. Sberbank spent a week finding the words to express its take on the situation. "Nine months of negotiation, a 9,000-page contract all set to be signed, and two days before the deal is set to go through, GM pulls out," fumed Gref to news channel *Vesti 24*. He threatened the Americans with legal action.

However, it didn't come to that. Karamzin claimed that the bank received more than adequate compensation from the Americans "for a deal whose collapse is unprecedented in international law". The press reported anonymous sources quoting €13 million — four and a half times less than the bank allegedly should have received as compensation for costs incurred, both direct and indirect. "I invested a fair amount of my own time in this", Gref reminded shareholders. The president's words, uttered shortly after the collapse of the deal, belied his frustration and anger. Would Gref simply accept defeat? Was the bank now finished with attempting such acquisitions? Quite the opposite, in fact: they were only just beginning.

CHAPTER 19
BUYING TIME

EARLY ON IN HIS CAREER, RUBEN VARDANIAN HAD struggled with the temptation to follow the easy money. The graduate student of Moscow State University's economics department would spend his morning commutes to the office — a one-room apartment with little more than a telephone, computer and a set of blinds — training himself to disregard the fast bucks being raked in by those around him. At that time, nobody was giving much thought to whether the deals being made were above board, or whether accounting was in line with international standards. In this respect, however, Vardanian preferred to be the black sheep. He chose to build a proper Western-style business in the decidedly improper 1990s. Years later, Vardanian expressed to me how grateful he would always be to Peter Derby, founder of investment firm Troika Dialog, for having given him his chance. Derby's investment of $35,000 did not come with any demands for quick returns — instead, the US financier, who had Russian ancestry, simply asked for a viable, reputable investment bank in exchange for his money.

Derby remained patient. He turned a blind eye to losses in the first year totalling $25,000, and did not pressure Vardanian for improvements. This cooperation between investor and Vardanian, a gifted manager, eventually began to bear fruit. Thanks to Derby's modest investment and invaluable guidance, a company emerged that, 20 years on, would be valued at $1 billion. Derby sold his shares in the 1990s, and thereafter continued to follow Troika's evolution as an outside observer, though with no less affection for the project. Troika did well from the voucher privatisation of the early '90s, but the firm really came into its own when the Russian Trading System was launched in 1995, becoming one of its most active brokers. The following year, Euromoney magazine named Troika Russia's best investment company. Soon, 85% of the Top 200 corporations could be counted among its clientèle. Long before the opening of the Skolkovo business school, which Vardanian would eventually end up running, MBA courses were already using the investment firm for case studies, one of which was titled "Ruben Vardanian at the helm of Troika Dialog". Students were, among other things, required to understand how the wily Vardanian had been able to buy back shares in Troika from the Bank of Moscow for virtually the same amount the bank had originally paid for them. In 1997, Bank of Moscow had acquired 80% of the company; five years later, the firm was reacquired in a management buy-out. "The investment business can and should be independent," Ruben had said at the time. However, he would soon come to revise this opinion.

The business quickly made a workaholic of Vardanian. He allowed himself five hours' sleep a night, and wouldn't take a day off for weeks on end. Even the New Year, which the rest of the country spent in a state of blissful relaxation, was normally celebrated at his desk. It was one such day during the January festivities that he first told me of the possibility of forming a partnership with Sberbank. Was this a prediction, or more likely the logical progression of his thinking?

CHAPTER 19 • BUYING TIME

Leaning back in his stiff office chair, Ruben, in his usual stately manner, elucidated the prospects for the business he had built. He envisaged three basic scenarios. The first — to become part of an international investment bank, an option he'd already ruled out. The next path was to remain independent and grow at market rate. This wasn't the worst idea, by any means. Market forecasts had been promising, and most importantly, were proving accurate. That year, the RTS index rose, and in the following year (2005) began to climb at a dizzying rate, increasing two-fold over the previous year's results (83.3%). But competition in an open market meant the future could never be certain. Global investment firms, which cast covetous glances towards Russia, proved a constant source of anxiety. Finally, the third scenario involved forming a sustainable financial holding company. "To do that, we need a partner," Ruben mused. "The question is — who? Who would be up to the task? Sberbank and Vneshtorgbank have plenty of staying power. However, we don't know what kind of strategic goals state shareholders would set for them."

By the end of the 1990s, Vardanian was sure that Sberbank offered the most potential as a partner in creating the Russian investment bank. Ruben even had talks with Andrei Kazmin, though evidently made little headway. Those at the state bank weren't especially moved by the idea of offering investment services. In the middle of the 2000s, Bella Zlatkis had been surprised to learn about the size of portfolio the bank's trust management services had to work with: 100 million roubles from just over 100 clients (by way of comparison, Troika Dialog's own trust management services were dealing with tens of billions of roubles). It's also worth noting that this sum, laughably small by industry standards, was managed not by one individual, but by a team of eight brokers.

A few years later, Sberbank came under new management. The incoming team now sought an investment company fit to become an integral part of the bank. A year had passed since GM's spectacular about turn, and the dizzy optimism of that period was now being subsumed by the daily grind of running the huge bank. The bank had been forced to move on, but it had not left its money, reputation and ambition behind.

Andrei Donskikh was another of those surprised by Sberbank's low profile in the investment market. For a number of years, he'd been head of Uralsib, which by 2010 was among the top ten private banks in Russia. Sberbank decided to offer the stocky, good-natured man, with his rich baritone voice, an opportunity to put his mind to work reviving a business that had been in protracted decline. Tariffs for precisely the same services could differ by a factor of fifteen from one branch to the next, even when both were on the same street. Companies with no reason to be turned down still had to wait up to six months for loan applications to be approved by the bank's enormous bureaucratic machine (other applications had to go through no less than five separate lending committees for consideration, a rigmarole that doubtless left a lasting impression on clients). Gref was desperate for Donskikh to deliver Sberbank from this absurdity as quickly as possible. Gref's incredulity when Donskikh requested four months' leave before taking up his new job was, therefore, understandable.

Donskikh loved travelling, and managed to wangle two months out of Gref, a period he spent in Australia and New Zealand. However, even on the

---

"Believe me, not everything depends on how close a bank is to the state. Small but solid banks can still do well."

Interview with German Gref, *Kommersant* (23.01.2012).

banks of picturesque Lake Rotorua, the banker still had business on his mind, occasionally jotting down ideas in his diary. "I'm making a work plan," he told his wife when caught with pen in hand. Considering he'd not spent so much as a day in the new job, how much of a plan could it have been? "You don't know what's there and what isn't," his surprised wife told him. "I know what should be there," was Donskikh's curt reply, before going back to his diary.

Sberbank wanted an investment business — the best, or at least the biggest, on the Russian market. Europe's leading banks, HSBC and BNP Paribas, both boasted their own examples. After the repeal of the Glass-Steagall Act, which for 66 years following the Great Depression required US banks to be exclusively investment or commercial, having an investment subsidiary became *de rigueur* for big banks in the United States. Sberbank saw itself among the big boys of global banking in the future, so if that was what was in fashion, the Russian giant wanted in on it too.

By not having a defined investment wing, Sberbank was losing out. Explosive growth was forecast in the IPO market. By the dozen, major companies were announcing plans to float on the stock market. It was virtually the same story with the domestic bond market, which was rapidly gaining momentum. According to Gref, without a strong investment wing, Sberbank could not consider itself a "full-fledged financial supermarket." To put it another way, it was missing out on a chance to make money. "As soon as the crisis began to unfold, our share of private equity portfolios grew sharply. As soon as it began to pass, our best clients, those who offered risk-free or low-risk returns, started leaving us. That's what's happening now: we're losing our largest, most reliable clients. They're going to the international markets," Gref explained to shareholders. What about services for collective investments? In India, the number of mutual funds per capita was five and a half times higher than in Russia. America was a given: the number of mutual funds there was 1,800 times higher. Meanwhile, the market for derivatives such as options, so popular in the West, was still in its infancy in Russia.

As usual, Sberbank had to play catch-up. Its reform programme had begun far later than it should have scheduled, and the investment side of the business lagged just as far behind. The bank lacked the experience, the clients, and the reputation in a notoriously fickle investment market to take the lead. The only thing Sberbank could count on was money: an abundance in that area allowed the bank to save on another vital strategic resource — time. Creating, developing and launching its own investment business, one capable of competing with market leaders, would require years of organic growth. A merger, on the other hand, could hurry things along nicely.

Vardanian was not the only option for Sberbank. Parallel discussions were also taking place with Renaissance Capital, another investment company of Russian origin, who in many senses were on a par with Troika. Two years previously, a 50% stake in the investment bank founded in Moscow by New Zealander Stephen Jennings and his partners was acquired by billionaire Mikhail Prokohorov's Onexim Group. Jennings remained in charge and continued as part-owner of a business that had spent 15 years in Russia. Sberbank knew it was a safe acquisition, but was in no hurry to seal the deal. The bank could expect to take complete control of Renaissance's counterparts at Troika, if not immediately, then in the near future. Full ownership was a key condition for the bank, and this was bound to be reflected in the terms of acquisition. However, unlike with Troika, the bank was wholly unable to come to any agreement over the full sale of Renaissance.

Troika, on the other hand, fitted what Sberbank was looking for in a number of parameters. Given the prestige and standing of the company, bringing Troika on board would guarantee Sberbank an opportunity to carve its way through the investment banking market like a knife through butter. It was a shot in the arm for the assets management and securities transaction sector. Shortly before the acquisition, Sberbank had created its own management company, but this did not generate as much excitement as the Troika partnership. Immediately prior to the sale, Vardanian's company was the largest mutual fund manager in Russia. Sberbank Asset Management, on the other hand, wasn't even in the top 20. It was a similar story at MICEX: Troika was among the top five for trading volume, while Sberbank didn't make the top ten.

Even before the acquisition, Gref and Vardanian had known each other through the Skolkovo business school, the Russia-Singapore Business Forum, and other projects. According to colleagues, the working relationship had long since become a personal friendship. Gref was, and remained, a man of the state, and Vardanian moved in similar circles. This canny character, fond of adopting a sombre expression across his bearded visage, was equally at home stalking the corridors of power as he was in the world of business.

Thanks to close cooperation with state company Russian Technologies, and its boss, Viktor Chemzov,

> "During discussions about the deal, ten principles of negotiation were formulated, and each was strictly adhered to. One of these was a system of meritocracy, whereby leadership positions would be awarded to the most capable people, regardless of their socio-economic backgrounds."
>
> Interview with Ruben Vardanian, *Kommersant* (03.05.2011).

whose family wealth was managed by Troika, Vardanian's investment company acquired stakes in vehicle producers Kamaz and AvtoVAZ. Later, the price of a blocking stake in AvtoVAZ purchased by Renault was valued at $1 billion. After Troika's whirlwind romance with the state, a deal with Russia's largest state bank seemed a logical way to bless the union. "In our case, one plus one will equal five," Varadanian assured the press at a conference to announce the conclusion of negotiations.

The parties disagreed over some of the terms of the deal (primarily the price), as well as the mechanisms for its conclusion, but bigger problems lay ahead. Any experienced mergers and acquisitions expert will tell you that the most difficult part of the process lies in merging disparate workforces, values, working styles, schedules, and anything else that constituted the typical working life of a company pre-merger. One or two politically insensitive moves and the old Armenian joke about crossing a hedgehog and a snake and getting barbed wire would no longer be a laughing matter. This had been borne out by experience all over the world: "80% of deals like this have ended in failure," Gref cautioned.

Troika was considered a large organisation in its own sector. It had 1,200 people working in Moscow and 20 other cities in Russia, as well as offices in New York, London, Kyiv, Nicosia and Alma-Ata. At Sberbank, there were three branches for every one of these specialists working with corporate clients. The bank's headquarters at 19 Vavilov Street alone could accommodate twice as many employees as the entire workforce of Troika. Vardanian pleaded that the difference in size between the companies not be made an issue. He quickly formed a good professional relationship with his immediate superior at Sberbank. When I asked him how working with Donskikh was, he flashed me a brief smile and raised his thumb. "We resolve any issues within a day, two at most," Ruben told *Kommersant*. "We decided that anything submitted to us had to be met with a 'yes' or 'no' within 24 hours."

But if major differences in working style were not felt at the top, they certainly were at the lower echelons. One manager who had worked with management at Troika prior to the merger compared it to mixing energy drinks with a milkshake: "Troika was full of swaggering alpha males," he had said, sharing his observations on condition of anonymity. "You could see some of them cruising around Moscow on Harley Davidsons. They treated clients like punchbags. Compared to them, we were a bunch of dorky accountants."

It wasn't simply a case of clashing temperaments. Having previously only worked in commercial banks, Donskikh was taken aback by how poorly trained some of the older hands at the state bank actually were. These experts working in international markets had no command of English. The simplest issues had them stuck, as if they'd never so much as opened a finance textbook. The 45-year-old Donskikh felt awkward working with brokers who'd started working for Sberbank when he'd still been at school. "I didn't expect to come across people in our sector who'd been in the same place for 30 years," he admitted to me. "They've spent all these years in this gated community, convinced there is no life beyond the walls of Vavilov Street." Donskikh saw no reason to hold on to these old cadres, and called for decisive action. It was a subject he'd argued long and hard over with Gref, who

> "Investment banking is not a market where two elephants can square up while the mice scuttle around the walls. Investment banking is not a market for administrative resources and money; it's a market for talent, for quality of service, for offering innovative investment products and programmes, and the competencies of those who work in these banks."
>
> Sberbank deputy chairman Andrey Donskikh's on *Ekho Moskvy* (15.03.2011).

seemed inclined to take a more conciliatory line on the matter. The bank's boss did not want an otherwise straightforward and transparent deal to be marred by bickering in a workforce where a healthy mental environment was important; Donskikh later stated that the bank had been able to maintain the bulk of its core staff after the merger.

However, there would come a time when Troika's restive staff would have to be tamed. The grizzled wolf of the investment business was used to playing by its own rules. Sberbank, weighed down by the twin millstones of state control and its own vast bulk, threatened to become a burden for free-spirited traders and market analysts. To avoid any nasty surprises, the bank made efforts to keep the seller on side throughout the deal. The $1 billion offered for Troika barely exceeded its nominal value (the company's net worth was valued at $872 million). Subsequently, the bank agreed to pay additional remuneration to Standard Life (the South African bank that owned just over a third of Troika's shares) and 130 other partners led by Vardanian. This sum would be tied to whatever profits Troika had made at the end of three years. For companies offering financial services, these kinds of incremental schemes were not unusual. This reduced the risk of key staff members — the investment business's main assets — leaving the company before the subsumed company had been fully integrated. To ensure some degree of continuity, the buyer added another important provision to the conditions of the deal: Troika, now in Sberbank's hands, would remain under Vardanian's stewardship until all terms of the takeover had been met.

Gref understood that integration would not be a painless process, just like many of the other initiatives he'd supported, and that the bank would suffer some mental anguish as a result. The two companies had very different success stories and equally differing degrees of professional independence. "Even a year ago, we wouldn't have been able to carry out a deal like this because of our complete mental unreadiness," Gref told *Kommersant*. "To be honest, this is another big test for us."

The acquisition of Troika was the final part of the puzzle for Sberbank's investment banking ambitions. But it now meant there was no going back. For the first time, the heir to the Soviet savings bank had absorbed a private company with which it had nothing in common (other than their respective managements' views on joint enterprise). A merger with one of the market's most successful players strengthened management's confidence that the days of the old Sberbank, passive and complacent, were now numbered.

CHAPTER 20
ISN'T IT JUST US?

IN THE LEAD-UP TO SBERBANK'S 170TH ANNIVERSARY, the bank launched a large-scale advertising campaign. Kitschy scenes from the pre-revolutionary era of the bank flashed all over prime-time broadcasts. One of them, it seemed to me, was not without a certain amount of self-deprecatory irony: a 19th century financial dignitary standing before a large map of the Russian Empire shares with a young colleague his plans for rolling out internet banking across the country. The short monologue is rounded off with a phrase about the vital importance of innovation. Why was innovation so important? "To be Russia's number one bank." His colleague is clearly taken aback by such a strange response: "But isn't it just us?"

This stereotype had become deeply rooted in the public consciousness. For most people, Sberbank *was* banking. Easy access to branches was a key factor — the old management had believed this was why customers remained loyal to the bank, forsaking all others. Wherever you went, there was Sberbank — one just round the corner, one near your home, another beside your work, a branch in every one-horse town. It was an advantage that outweighed anything the others could offer, be it a pleasant retail environment, one-on-one attention, or simple and efficient service. For years, Sberbank had been happy to let its customers fume impotently in queues, to be rude and surly in interactions with them, and essentially leave them under no illusions as to how little they meant to the bank as individuals. Regardless, Sberbank was where people went whenever they needed to make payments or transfers. According to surveys conducted by the National Agency for Financial Studies in 2007, 64% of respondents trusted state banks with their savings, with over half naming Sberbank specifically. Over subsequent years, the picture didn't change significantly: Sberbank continued to be the place where the nation preferred to keep its money.

The Russian banking industry is configured in a unique way; it is inhabited by a thousand Davids and only one Goliath. Bankers who had worked with commercial banks and had subsequently moved to Sberbank recalled how they had treated the giant as a statistical aberration; in every market chart, the bank was off the scale. With the leviathan taken out of calculations, the market instantly seemed more balanced, and each of the next 100 banks less insignificant.

The next largest state-controlled bank, VTB, was more of a partner to Sberbank than a rival. In any case, each bank was fighting in complete different weight categories; Sberbank's assets were over twice those of VTB's, whose retail chain made up only a fortieth of what had been passed on from the former Soviet savings bank. At one stage, Pochta-Bank was considered a potential rival, with the new bank to be based on the post office network and the Vnesheconombank-owned Sviaz-Bank chain. However, with each passing year, the project's prospects of success have looked increasingly bleak.

What kind of competition did foreign banks offer? Once upon a time, their arrival in Russia filled local bankers with dread. Even Kazmin had come out

> "Today, we're one of the most significant financial institutions in the world."
>
> Interview with German Gref, Channel *Dozhd*, (02.02.2012).

in support of the government as it was defending its restriction of the activities of foreign banks during negotiations on accession to the WTO, agreeing to permit subsidiaries to operate only under the strict control of the Russian banking regulator. In 2002, there were 27 such banks in the country, controlling 5.4% of Russian financial assets. By 2007, there were 61 operational foreign banks in Russia, but the influence they exerted remained minimal, controlling 10% of assets between them. Over the 20 years of post-communist capitalism in Russia, the West, despite its centuries of banking experience, could not make any headway against the state banks, primarily Sberbank. This sharply contrasted with the expansion of global business in the markets of the other eastern European countries. Skandinavska Enskilda Banken, along with Swedbank, had long ruled the roost in the Baltic markets. Their investments in Latvia, Lithuania and Estonia reached as much as a fifth of these countries' GDPs. The Czech Republic, Hungary, Slovakia, Croatia, Romania, Serbia… everywhere was dominated by Western capital. As far back as the 1990s, Poland was so overrun by Western bankers that two-thirds of deposits and three-quarters of the loans in the country were under their control.

It was a different picture altogether in Russia. Despite the multitude of foreign banks, their market share of retail deposits and loans never exceeded 1%. This situation suited neither their shareholders nor management. As such, the Western bankers quietly upped sticks and left. Europe's largest bank, HSBC, maintained only its corporate business in Russia. Santander's last retail office in Moscow also kicked the bucket. Neither Barclays nor Swedbank thought it worthwhile developing a retail presence in Russia.

CHAPTER 20 • ISN'T IT JUST US?

Morgan Stanley, having acquired CityMortgage Bank on the back of a wave of interest in mortgage services, quickly offloaded it. The list of failed incursions is long, and in all probability, likely to grow further.

It must have been lonely for Sberbank, up on its pedestal all by itself. In numerous interviews, the bank's management flexed their muscles, demonstrating their invincibility to these unseen enemies. But who were they? "Who is our main rival for the nation's savings?" was the rhetorical question posed by Valentin Mikhov of the department for strategy and development.

Sberbank's previous management was about as concerned by the subject of competition as it was by magnetic storms on Mars, but it was nonetheless aware of a force that rivalled even the bank for influence — the cash dollar. Immediately after the August 1998 crash, the US currency demonstrated to the average Russian its ability to rise several times against the rouble over the course of a few weeks. The banks had made it difficult or, at times, even impossible for depositors to access their own accounts, something that made the space underneath the floorboards even more attractive as an alternative vault for their deposits.

A decade of relative calm went some way to restoring confidence in the banks. But for the largest of them, the main enemy remained cash. Gref was determined to go on the offensive. The amount of hard cash kept by Russians was approaching 12% of GDP, twice as much as in the US and four times more than Britons, the Swiss, and South Koreans. Russia even lagged behind comparable economies such as Brazil and Mexico. When in 2009, the European Central Bank ranked 28 European countries by the number of non-cash transactions carried out by their populace over the course of a year, Russia came in fourth from

> "I'd like to see Sberbank on an international level: for such an enormous bank, the market in a country as large as Russia is still a cramped one."
>
> Interview with German Gref, *Vedomosti*, (26.09.2008).

the bottom. The average Russian paid for goods and services by card or mobile phone 14 times less often than his counterpart in Finland, though did so twice as often as the Greeks and three times more than Bulgarians. Gref spoke of the colossal losses created by an economy that was overloaded with cash; according to Sberbank's estimates, these were in the region of 0.9 trillion roubles (2.3% of GDP) in net costs, taking into account missed income from interest payments. For Sberbank, this was primarily money it was not able to make anything from. Cash payments in Russia were supposed to become a thing of the past, subsumed by the march of progress that the bank was so desperate to be leading.

Sberbank decided to get proactive, and was one of those involved in the development of the Universal Electronic Card. The project aimed to encourage a gradual change in the way Russians thought about money. According to its developers, the Universal Card was to serve both as a means of identification and also as a way of paying for a wide range of services, including passage on public transport. Naturally, it was also to feature a banking application, offering potential for increased income from commission fees and near unlimited opportunities for selling and testing credit products. Gref wanted to go further, and Sberbank called for the laws to be refined: why not transfer all salaries, benefits and pensions to bankcards? How long would retail — from hypermarkets to kiosks — be permitted to refuse card payments? Gref's initiative was not met by much enthusiasm by either officials or business figures. However, the war was not yet lost.

The bank was only just venturing into the hi-tech sphere, and in a broader sense was now beginning to act in a commensurate fashion to its size and status.

> "I myself still carry cash alongside the cards in my pocket."
>
> Interview with German Gref, Forbes Kazakhstan, (11.2011).

Gref told me that Sberbank's services were used by over half the population: "We have 70 million customers, while the state has 140 million. It's twice as much, not ten times." Moreover, the bank was beginning to go global, and no longer in the figurative sense. In spring 2010, Sberbank joined British market research agency Millward Brown's list of the 100 most valuable international brands, and for the next two years rubbed shoulders with Wall Street stalwarts such as Citigroup, J.P. Morgan Chase and Goldman Sachs. However, the best indicator of having attained supranational status was when the bank's management actively began to expand its horizons and lay the groundwork for foreign deals.

Andrei Kazmin had been sceptical of going beyond the boundaries of the former Soviet Union. Ukraine or Kazakhstan was no problem, since the bank was able to offer customers there 'the standard service'. Kazmin spoke of how Sberbank had received offers "from serious institutions" to open offices in the US and Europe, but had politely declined them. An open representative office in the Czech Republic also had to be turned down. "The EU is a huge problem, and there are a thousand reasons why we can't do it", Kazmin told *Ekho Moskvy*.

Gref had a different outlook altogether. By 2008, it was already apparent that Sberbank was keen to spread its wings. The bank's five-year strategy made this clear: no less than 5-7% of its business was eventually to come from foreign countries. In the long term — in 20 to 30 years — Gref hoped to increase revenue generated from overseas assets to 50% of the bank's total. Integration into the global market reduced the bank's vulnerability to domestic shocks, or as bankers would put it, hedged its risks. The Russian Central Bank was largely

> "Yesterday I had the president of one of the world's largest international banks with me, and he said that our situation is one of the best in the industry, that our stability indicators are the stuff of dreams. And it's true."
>
> Interview with German Gref, *Vedomosti*, (11.11.2011).

sympathetic to such plans. International development actually made the regulator's position less ambiguous. Domestic banking regulation by the Central Bank usually presented something of a conflict of interests, since it also happened to be the main shareholder in the market's biggest player. Now, however, its 'subsidiary' was intent on building an overseas network. Domestic monopolism was thereby transformed into the rather more palatable concept of creating a proper Russian multinational bank, one that would rival the largest in the world.

The idea seemed rather grand, and it took time to be accepted. Were there many Russian banks willing to step up and do their bit to develop a 21st-century financial system integrated into the global market? Were they ready to make it official strategy, instead of the usual half-baked agreements made at drunken banquets? Yuri Ismagilov, acting chairman of the Mid-Russian Bank of Sberbank, recalled the wide-eyed incredulity of his colleagues, regional bosses, when they first heard of these positively Napoleonic ambitions: "Most couldn't get their heads round why such internationalisation was necessary," he said. "We should first be working out how to provide a proper service to OAPs, then move on to world domination."

But the decision had been made. Sberbank opened up representative offices in Germany and China, launched a branch in India, and put plans in place to enter the market in Turkey and Poland. The watershed moment occurred in Vienna, the magnificent city being the scene of Sberbank's purchase of Volksbank International, a division of Osterreichische Volksbanken-AG group, for €505 million (the initial price having been lowered by €80 million, to the delight of the buyer).

Its title was fitting: Volksbank really was the 'people's' bank. It had been founded in the mid-19th century as a credit union whose members lent to one another, as well as providing a place to deposit their savings. Its area of influence was defined by the boundaries of those nations that had once partially or fully been part of the Austro-Hungarian Empire, and was headquartered in the empire's former metropolis, Vienna. Sberbank bought up the group's Eastern European business, which included banks in Bosnia-Herzegovina, Hungary, Serbia, Slovakia, Slovenia, the Czech Republic, Croatia and Ukraine. Assets in Romania were not included in the deal, as they were deemed too likely to cause problems: indeed, Romania was the only country in which the bank was chronically unable to turn a profit.

Even then, Volksbank's success in other countries was hardly resounding. After their acquisition of Ukraine's Elektrobank, the bank couldn't even make the top 50 credit institutions in the country (its Russian division had its license revoked in 2000). Overall, the previous decade wasn't the most glorious in Volksbank's history, and it barely survived the financial crash. It was able to claw back €272 million from the sale of property company Europolis AG, but was still forced to merge with Osterreichische Volksbanken. However, the problems didn't end here. Financial authorities still had doubts about the stability of the company. After the sale of Volksbank to Sberbank had gone through, news came through from debt-blighted Europe that the seller of the controlling stake, Osterreichische Volksbanken-AG, had failed stress tests designed to determine the endurance of the banking system in the event of a severe economic downturn in the Eurozone.

The group's disheartened management claimed that they'd been shot down by the regulator on take-off: inspectors had not taken into account the deal with the Russians, or Osterreichische Volksbanken-AG's merger with another Austrian bank, Investkredit. Volksbank was far from the finished article, as its buyer freely admitted: "The level of development in many of their processes left a lot to be desired, and a number of them needed to be created from scratch", said deputy chairman Sergei Gorkov, who, along with personnel policy, oversees Sberbank's international operations. Gref looked tired but pleased when he announced the acquisition in Moscow: "Yes, it's tough for European banks at the moment. But frankly, we're making the most of the situation." In an interview he later gave to *Die Presse* in Vienna, he steered clear of any bold statements. To questions about plans for further expansion, he replied that he wasn't keen on the word 'expansion'. Sberbank would move into the market "gradually and gently". The Eastern European states had no great affection for Russia. From a distance, it was easy to draw parallels between Soviet tanks on the streets of Budapest and Prague and the giant Russian bank — an uninvited guest muscling in on someone else's financial system. Sberbank tried not to arouse any more concern. This meant no bragging and no challenging local regulators or public sentiment. "Look at the banks we've bought," Gref said by way of reassurance. "It'll take scrupulous effort and a lot of time to bring them up to a decent technological standard. It'll be years before we're at a point where we have a significant market share."

In the meantime, Sberbank had already hatched plans to buy the Turkish DenizBank, founded during the presidency of Mustafa Kemal Atatürk as a means to finance the maritime industry in the fledgling republic. DenizBank was certainly not top dog in Turkey, accounting for only 2.8% of all deposits in the country, and was barely among the top ten Turkish banks for assets. Volksbank's position was no more impressive: it was, at best, third in its own market. This was unfamiliar territory for Sberbank — what did it mean to be third, or worse, tenth, in a highly competitive field? It was impossible for the Russian giant to imagine.

Long before the sweltering autumn of 2007, when there was still no indication of the upheaval that lay ahead, the banking market had enjoyed idly musing about what would become of Sberbank were it a different beast altogether: modern, dynamic, client-oriented, and with a business model along international lines. As vibrant as a peacock's tail, it would spell the end for Russia's banking system. Were Sberbank able to offer quality service and products in its thousands of branches, it would render most other credit institutions redundant and even less stable than they already were. Russian banks' capacity to collapse like a house of cards was evident from their numbers: over the last 15 years, after a couple of crises, their numbers decreased by two and half times, and this decline slowly continued.

The changes at Sberbank had inevitably changed the market itself. If the bank so much as sneezed, the echo was deafening. Major transformations that proved successful there meant bad news for everyone else.

Nonetheless, it is fair to say there is still a long way to go. Customers still find the state bank a cold and insensitive place, and they haven't been especially blown away by first round of improvements. Just as in the good old days, phones are left to ring unanswered.

> "If I relax, that's when you'll see a relaxed Sberbank."
>
> Interview with German Gref, Forbes, (21.03.2012).

The contrast between the unrelenting crush in Sberbank's branches and the tranquil offices of the commercial banks continues to be a striking one. It will take years of hard work to rectify this state of affairs in the larger cities alone.

Russians have always preferred the sprint to the marathon — they don't have the stamina. As a result, reform is always a risky business. They need a strong leader who can keep things under control. "Am I satisfied?", Gref responded with surprise when asked whether he was pleased with the progress the bank had made. "No, no, no — I'm not satisfied with anything. As soon as I'm satisfied with everything, you can assume it's time for me to move on."

Will Sberbank finally claim victory over the long queues? Will it teach its staff to love and understand their customers? Will it earn a place among the pantheon of the world's greatest banks? Even if despite all efforts, not everything it endeavours to achieve succeeds, the very attempt to change the course of history at Russia's largest bank deserves respect. It is a bank that embodies all of the hereditary defects of Russian society, chief among them the reluctance to embrace change, and the rejection of anything that goes beyond personal experience. Now, change has become part of that experience, an experience shared by hundreds of thousands of employees. As a result, Sberbank can look forward to a future in which it can be anything it wants to be, but it cannot go back. It has passed the point of no return. The elephant is not dancing quite yet. But it now knows the steps.

ACKNOWLEDGEMENTS

FIRSTLY, I WOULD LIKE TO THANK THE JOURNALIST Sergei Kashin, together with whom I began work on this book, and who conducted many of the interviews used herein. We discussed the idea behind the book at great length, and in the course of these conversations he shared with me his thoughts on banking, a subject of which he has an infinitely greater understanding than I do. For personal reasons, Sergei decided to leave the project and allow me to carry on the book alone. I sincerely appreciate the assistance he was able to provide.

There is another person without whom this book truly would not have happened. Maxim Kotin not only inspired me to embark on a venture that I still consider to be an attempt to condense in a relatively short text the incomprehensibly enormous transformation of a banking empire, but his editorial criticism has also been the most insightful and cogent I've experienced in all my years as a journalist. It has been invaluable. His countless tips and editorial observations have allowed me to fill important conceptual gaps in the manuscript and make it a more logical and substantive piece. Or at least, I consider it such.

I am also indebted to the head of Mann, Ivanov & Ferber, Mikhail Ivanov, who steered me towards writing the book well before the project's outset.

I am grateful to the staff at Sberbank's public relations department for their assistance in organising dozens of meetings with the bank's senior managers — extremely busy people who didn't always understand the nature of my interest in them. Of course, not all would have agreed to meet with me, had they not been asked in the right way. For this, I offer separate thanks to vice-president Yuri Rovensky. I am also grateful to Andrei Zaionets, former employee of the same department, for his organisational efforts. Alexei Volodkin provided me with a wealth of interesting information. I certainly owe a huge debt of thanks to Pavel Fomin — I would not have got far without his connections within the bank's head office, energetic support, and fastidiously collected archive material. Yulia Shelegova, head of the Moscow Sberbank's press centre, also provided invaluable assistance.

I would also like to thank my colleagues Irina Stolyarova and Alexander Kiyatkin for drawing my attention to some interesting facts from Gref's past and Sberbank's present.

My wife and children have stoically endured my dive into the deep waters of literary creation, and it would be remiss of me not to make some simple expression of my gratitude to them. My five-year-old son would often ask me what I was doing on my laptop instead of helping him with his Lego sets. "Writing your book, I suppose?" he would mutter, without waiting for a response. I indulge myself with the faint hope that at some point in the future, he'll be interested in what his father eventually produced.

At the end of the book, I have attempted to list the sources of all quotes and facts taken from media, literature, blogs, etc. The rest is drawn from the testimonies of Sberbank's staff and management, including German Gref, from materials provided by the bank, and from my own work as a journalist over the past 15 years.

NOTES

Insomnia

PAGE 9: *Knowing the weakness Viktor Gerashchenko, former head of the Central Bank, had for plain speaking, journalists badgered him for his thoughts, and he duly obliged: replacing Kazmin with Gref could turn out to be a foolish move.* – Viktor Gerashchenko: "Zamena Kaz'mina na Grefa okazhetstya glupost'yu" // DP.RU 07.10.2007

PAGE 10: *He later complained that he had been tricked by Moscow mayor Yuri Luzhkov...* – N. Krotov. Sberbank – eto bank kotory mozhet vse // Bankir.ru 25.01.2010

PAGE 10: *A motley crew of bankers and politicians had been tipped for Kazmin's desk...* – Y. Albats. Kiriyenko: chto eto bylo? // Kommersant. 17.10.1998; Vladmir Kogan mozhet vozglavit' Sberbank Rossii? // Online publication "Bokrug novostei". 17.05.2005.

PAGE 12: *"In rugby it's not done for players to argue with the referee," Kazmin enthusiastically told an in-house magazine. "Only the team captain can speak to the referee and only with the referee's permission. The captain himself cannot approach the referee. The referee conducts the game with a radio relay. He has a transmitter and his entire team are audible to the crowd."* – D. Simonov, O. Kameneva, V Karpinskaya. Itogi s Andreem Kaz'minym // Pryamye investitsii. 2007. November.

PAGE 15: *"In no country in the world would a rational government consider such a move", he bristled. "Why kill the goose that lays the golden eggs?"* – Ibid.

PAGE 15: *In 2001 the main objective was not to capture hearts and minds, but "to preserve the position of a modern, first-rate, competitive bank, the largest in Eastern Europe."* – Sberbank's Concept of Development to 2005.

PAGE 15: *More than 204,000 people worked for the bank in the period leading up to 2002...* – Sberbank's annual report for 2001. p. 42.

PAGE 15: *...and six years later this number had exceeded 262,000.* – Annual report of Sberbank JSC for 2007.

PAGE 15: *In 2007, Sberbank's piece of the pie reached 5 trillion roubles.* – Ibid.

PAGE 16: *..."a thrift institution system",...* – I. Petrov. Tantsy so slonami // Kommersant Dengi. 03.12.2007.

PAGE 16: *..."guaranteed a growth in profit returns of 25-30% yearly".* – D. Simonov, O. Kameneva, V Karpinskaya. Itogi s Andreem Kaz'minym // Pryamye investitsii. 2007. November.

PAGE 17: *"There is a very high strain on our operational apparatus – seven times more than Eastern Europe, and around ten times that of Western Europe. They have 1000-3000 clients per service point, while we have 30,000-40,000".* – I. Moiseev. Na tri goda sredstv ot razmeshcheniya vpolne khvatit // Kommersant. 29.06.2007.

PAGE 17: *Lord Victor Rothschild of the celebrated banking family saw the purpose of banks as "facilitating the movement of money from point A, where it is, to point B, where it is needed."* – Quotation from N. Ferguson. The Ascent Of Money: Penguin, 2008. It is interesting to note that this lapidary statement on the role of banks was made by a man who wanted no part in the family business. The 3rd Baron Rothschild was the first of Rothschild lords to turn his back on financing as a career (see Frederic Morton. The Rothschilds: Portrait of a Dynasty for more detail.)

PAGE 18: *The bank favoured major borrowers.*- Y. Berezanskaya. Krugovorot deneg // Forbes Russia. 2006. January.

PAGE 18: *However, as far back as 2002, Vadim Kleiner, Head of Research at British investment fund Hermitage Capital Management, who had joined Sberbank's supervisory board, publicly accused the bank of lending to major Russian corporations at undervalued rates.* – Y. Berezanskaya. Razoblacheniye "Sbera" // Vedomosti. 05.12.2002.

PAGE 20: *Kazmin explained this as his reluctance to take part in the extraordinary general meeting: "I'm leaving the bank, so it should be those who are staying that vote."* – D. Simonov, O. Kameneva, V Karpinskaya. Itogi s Andreem Kaz'minym // Pryamye investitsii. 2007. November.

The Main Strategist

PAGE 22: *German, the youngest in the family, grew up without a father.* – O. Larionova. Uzh osen' blizitsya, a Germana vse net // Sobesednik. 21.08.2001.

PAGE 23: *Gref, by his own admission, wasn't particularly concerned with formal elements of study such as grades.* – Sberbank epokhi peremen // Pryamye investitsii. 2011. January.

PAGE 24: *The second affirms that there had been a few blips along the way.* – Gref German Oskarovich – biografiya // Panorama Expert Information Group

PAGE 24: *Newspapers reported that he suffered a serious head injury and broke several vertebrae.* – E Bagaev. Rukovoditeli ingosimushchestva popali v avariyu // Kommersant. 19.01.1999.

PAGE 26: *Gref's boss endeavoured to breathe life into the city property sector for which he was responsible.* – Vecherny Peterburg. 18.09.1997.

PAGE 27: *Scandal even overshadowed the opening of a settlement for the descendants of Germans deported to Kazakhstan.* – A. Ivanitsky. Pod Grefom – "Sekretno" //

Novaya Gazeta. 29.05.2000; Radio Svoboda, Liberty Live programme. 17.10.2003 (http://www.svobodanews.ru/content/article/24187754.html)

PAGE 27: *Along with lowering poverty levels and reducing external debt as a means of supporting the state's creditworthiness, this was one of three goals later considered achieved...* – D. Butrin. Podvedeny itogi udvoeniya VVP // Kommersant. 02.06.2010.

PAGE 27: *(this was by no means the consensus view...)* – http://www.fbk.ru/news/5419/833760/

PAGE 28: *Ivanov once asked prime-minister Mikhail Fradkov, later director of the Foreign Intelligence Service, whether he really needed to show that the sole manufacturer of nuclear submarines in Russia (the Severodvinsk-based Sevmash) had no competitors in the country. "Not me. Gref. You need to show Gref", he replied.* – Sergei Ivanov khochet spasti armiyu ot importnoi tushenki // RIA Novosti. 13.05.2004.

PAGE 29: *"At a transitional stage of societal development, one must choose between democracy and economic progress"...* – Lee Kuan Yew. Singaporskaya istoriya: iz tret'ego mira – v pervy // MGIMO University, 2010.

PAGE 29: *By the end of the first decade of the 21st century, ministry officials such as deputy minister Andrei Klepach were beginning to admit publicly that the state controlled half the Russian economy, a figure many regarded as conservative.* – Minekonomrazvitiya otsenivaet gosdolyu v ekonomike RF na 50% // RIA Novosti. 02.07.2009.

PAGE 30: *Gref was the main lobbyist for Russia's accession to the WTO...* – A. Shapovalov. Kuriny oskal // Kommersant. 17.08.2006.

PAGE 30: *Years later, Gref admitted to journalists that part of the reason he couldn't remain in the service of the state was the "pittance" he earned: "I have young children, and I needed to earn enough to live on. Unless you have some kind of additional earnings, it's impossible to live on that money", he said in an interview with Forbes Kazakhstan.* – M. Semelyak. Strelochnik // Forbes Kazakhstan. 2011. November.

Strange Things

PAGE 35: *This figure "has no meaning other than the fact that it's big and round and makes something of an impression on a credulous mind", wrote one user of an unofficial blog for bank clerks.* – http://sber-bank.livejournal.com/387.html

PAGE 35: *"These distinguished consultants are used to working in countries where business is transparent and they don't need to double-check every figure. A few of them ended up offering their services, but came unstuck at the first task."* – A. Aleshkina. Vremya pokupat' aktsii Sberbanka // Pryamye investitsii. 2003. November.

PAGE 36: *In the 1960s, expressions such as 'to McKinsey'...* – Christopher McKenna. The World's Newest Profession: Management Consulting in the Twentieth Century // Cambridge University Press. 2006. p. 181.

PAGE 36: *By the 2000s, the company name was generally coupled with the word "elite" in business literature.* – This phenomenon is evident in, for example, Roger Lowenstein's book When Genius Failed: The Rise and Fall of Long-Term Capital Management // Random House. 2000.

PAGE 37: *As Christopher McKenna notes in his book...* – Christopher McKenna. The World's Newest Profession: Management Consulting in the Twentieth Century. p. 208.

PAGE 37: *In the spirit of Trudy Rubin's famous response to Vladimir Putin...* – The Philadelphia Enquirer journalist posed the now famous "Who is Mister Putin?" question to members of the Russian delegation at the Davos World Economic Forum in January 2000.

PAGE 38: *By 2007, less than a year before he arrived at the bank, the McKinsey partner had been featured in the magazine*

Finans as one of the most successful young businesspeople in Russia. – Reiting 33 samikh "krutykh pertsev" // Finans. 08.04.2007.

PAGE 38: *During a Q&A session with Siberian students on the subject of talent, motivation and careers, Denis Bugrov recalled that by his first year at university he was earning "considerably more than his bursary".* – Televised Q&A session with Sberbank senior managers. 12.09.2009. (http://www.sibnet.ru/bridge/?use=sberbank)

PAGE 38: *Denis Bugrov ended up in the Moscow office of McKinsey...* – McKinsey's Moscow office website, http://www.mckinsey.com/locations/moscow/ourpeople/alumni/

A Prison For Money

PAGE 45: *"The lessons of history must be heeded: empires that cannot adapt fall"...* – Letter from Gref to employees. 01.08.2008.

PAGE 47: *"We've no reason to blush", he told the magazine Kompaniya, "we'll learn what there is to learn, but we can report with pride on the products we offer that they can't. 'They' being developed countries."* – A. Grigoriev, A Kazmin. Sberbank – eto prazdnik, kotory vsegda s toboi // Kompaniya. 09.06.2003.

PAGE 48: *Upon buying Snoras, Antonov's first act was to commend the bank's retail technology – as his second, he announced plans for its wholesale improvement with the assistance of McKinsey...* – K. Yacheistov. Konversbank kupil litovsky Sberbank // Kommersant. 24.03.2003.

PAGE 48: *"This isn't a paper we hired some consultants to knock up for us"...* – Letter from Gref to employees. 05.03.2009.

PAGE 50: *...so that, as Gref hoped, "every employee recognises his place and his role in our common endeavour".* Letter from Gref to staff. 05.03.2009.

PAGE 50: *Consider, for instance, this passage from Kazmin's strategy: "The bank's long-standing experience of a large-scale client base and branch network, guaranteeing universal access to services, creates ... a basis for strengthening our leading position."* – Sberbank's Concept of Development to 2012. 2007. p. 9.

PAGE 50: *And here is the Gref alternative: "The poor exploitation of two competitive advantages of the bank: the marketing network and client base, [is a serious shortcoming]."* – Sberbank's Development Strategy up to 2014. 2008. p. 5.

PAGE 51: *The old management saw the task to be "increasing productivity"...* – Sberbank's Concept of Development to 2012. 2007. p. 8.

PAGE 51: *...but neglected to assess its current level – "singularly low"...* – Sberbank's Development Strategy up to 2014. 2008. p. 6.

PAGE 51: *For this, the bank intended to "free up resources for improving the quality of service and working more intensively with customers in selling banking products."* – Sberbank's Development Strategy up to 2014. 2008. p. 25.

PAGE 52: *Staff working structures had to be reorganised and personnel involved in the reform process with the assistance of a productive system that the management saw as "a new ideology of administration".* – Sberbank's Development Strategy up to 2014. 2008. p. 19.

Common Sense Is Always Wrong

PAGE 53: *"Does an American really make ten times the effort? Clearly, the Japanese are wasting their energies somewhere"...* – Taiichi Ohno. Proizvodstvennaya sistema Toyoty: Ukhodya ot massovogo proizvodstva // Institute for Complex Strategic Studies. 2005. p. 30.

PAGE 55: *"Common sense is always wrong", Taiichi Ohno loved to say.* – Daniel T. Jones and James P. Womack.

Lean Thinking: Banish Waste and Create Wealth in Your Corporation // Simon & Schuster. 2003. p. 233.

PAGE 56: *Ohno said that he'd sought out "a means of making production work for the company in the way a human body works for its occupant".* – Taiichi Ohno. Proizvodstvennaya systema Toyoty: Ukhodya ot massovogo proizvodstva // Institute for Complex Strategic Studies. 2005. p. 13.

PAGE 57: *"25 years ago, it was just one of a herd of Asian interlopers selling fuel-efficient econoboxes, and Detroit snickered at the notion that Americans would ever want to buy many of them. As everyone now knows, that crystal ball was cloudy: Toyota's Camry has been the bestselling car in the US since 2002, and the Lexus LS 430 has been the leading luxury-car brand for seven straight years."* – Anne Fisher. America's most admired companies // Fortune. 05.03.2007.

PAGE 58: *"This is the one advantage of those who are closest to death"...* – Interview with Taiichi Ohno. "New Production System: JIT Crossing Industry Boundaries", 1988. Quoted in Daniel T. Jones and James P. Womack. Lean Thinking: Banish Waste and Create Wealth in Your Corporation (Russian Translation) // Alpina Business Books. 2004. p. 292.

I Knew Nothing About Lean

PAGE 63: *"Otherwise, they generally fail or grind to a halt"...* – The full quote reads: "Generally, as a result of my subsequent state experience, I have come to the conclusion that in Russia, reforms must be carried out quickly and promptly, other they generally fail or grind to a halt." – S. Y. Witte. Vospominaniya. Vol. II. (Reign of Nicholas II) // Izdatel'stvo sotsial'no-ekonomicheskoi literatury, 1960. p. 94.

PAGE 65: *"It's really infectious. Workers are going home and implementing lean strategies there"...* – Ilya Zhigulev. Anastasia Ponomarenko, zaveduyushchaya lin-laboratoriyei Sberbanka: "My vse zarazilis' filosofiyei Lean" // Slon.

ru. 07.04.2009 (http://slon.ru/business/anastasiya_ponomarenko_zaveduyushhaya_lin_laborato-1959.xhtml)

PAGE 66: *The study "Lean production and disability"...* – Antoon Spithoven (Utrecht University School of Economics): "Lean Production and Disability" // International Journal of Social Economics. 2001. pp. 725-741.

PAGE 66: *"People's muscles had atrophied, their expressions blank, shoulders hunched – basically, they were on the edge of nervous collapse", was the picture one former employee of a Sberbank branch in Vladimir Oblast painted of the end of average day.* – http://178.248.232.19/services/official/bank/index.php?PAGEN_3=3&responseID=2924305

PAGE 66: *At the start of autumn 2008, he'd hurriedly assured staff that the system would be in place in every main branch by the end of the year, and for every member of staff by the middle of the next.* – Letter from Gref to employees.01.09.2008.

PAGE 67: *A study into the Russian retail sector conducted by McKinsey in 2009...* – Effektivnaya Rossiya. Proizvoditel'nost' kak fundament rosta. Section of " Proizvoditel'nost' roznichnogo bankovskogo sektora" // V. Klintsov, D. Popov, D. Tafintsev, I. Shvakman // McKinsey Global Institute. 2009. April. pp. 101-123.

PAGE 69: *Drucker knew that the world was nowhere near developing effective management methods for those who worked more with their heads than with their hands...* – P. Drucker. Zadachi menedzhmenta v XXI veke // Dialektika, 2002. pp. 190-200.

PAGE 69: *Responsibility for productivity, this "source of all economic values"...* – Peter Drucker quoted in D. Scott Sink. Upravleniye proizvoditel'nost'yu: planirovaniye, izmereniye i otsenka, kontrol' i povysheniye // Progress, 1989. p. 63.

PAGE 72: *"Forget everything you used to know about value"...* – Daniel T. Jones and James P. Womack. Lean Thinking: Banish Waste and Create Wealth in Your

Corporation (Russian translation) // Alpina Business Books. 2004. p. 52.

PAGE 73: *Together with colleague Guy Parsons, he took control of the struggling bicycle producer Merlin Metalworks in Cambridge, Massachusetts.* – Art Kleiner. "Leaning Toward Utopia" // Strategy+Business. 2005.

PAGE 74: *"For service companies, these programmes are not applicable", he had said. "Here's where the difficulty lies: there's no-one we can borrow a well-worked-out system from."* – Sberbank epokhi peremen // Pryamye investitsii. 2011. January.

PAGE 74: *In 2003, local partners of McKinsey unearthed evidence of particularly successful lean implementation by Chilean banks.* – Tomás Elewaut, Patricia Lindenboim, Damián L. Scokin. Chile's lesson in lean banking // McKinsey Quarterly. 2003. August.

PAGE 75: *Gref himself had been impressed by the way lean had helped centralise the back office functions of UniCredit.* – O. Proskurnina, B. Safronov, V. Kudinov. Sberbank ne monopolist // Vedomosti. 26.09.2008.

PAGE 76: *She was convinced that the production system offered the bank a "competitive advantage", which would make it possible to "raise the quality of service to world-class".* – "Ne menyayas' – my ugasayem" // Moi Sberbank. 03.06.2011.

PAGE 77: *Introduced in the 1980s by Tom Peters and Robert Waterman in their business bestseller, In Search of Excellence...* – Tom Peters and Robert H. Waterman, Jr.. In Search of Excellence (Russian Translation) // Alpina Publisher. 2010.

PAGE 77: *At McDonald's it had grown into a tradition – every 15th April, on the company's birthday, managers would leave their offices to spend a few hours at the coalface.* – Konstantin Poltev. Big Mac po-russki // Itogi. 01.08.2011.

PAGE 77: *Pointing to the silver-haired billionaire, the mother warned her son: "If you don't stick in at school, you'll end up like*

NOTES

that old man over there, packing people's shopping for them in your old age." – Lennart Dahlgren. Vopreki absurdu: kak ya pokoryal Rossiyu, a ona – menya // United Press, 2010. p. 119.

The 5S Deep Clean

PAGE 79: *"If you scrawl 'Sberbank' on a wall in chalk, about 30 pensioners will start queuing"...* – "Sberbank izvinilsya pered pensionerami za neudachnuyu shutku v Twitter" // Praim. 09.08.2012.

PAGE 83: *Gref said the same things, but in different units: "It's possible to use every square centimetre efficiently and effectively."* Letter from Gref to staff. 22.09.2010.

PAGE 84: *"Instead of rewriting the stupid instructions and cutting down on paperwork, SPS disciples are 'reshaping space and time' by moving tables around and doing time-motion studies", read one of the dreadfully libellous comments on the banking forums.*
- http://www.banki.ru/services/official/bank/index.php?responseID=2853554

PAGE 85: *"Today 5S got applied – everything got scrubbed with bleach", said one worker at a Moscow Sberbank about her branch's preparations for a planned inspection.* – http://storyonline.ru/story_1037/str_78.html

PAGE 85: *At head office, underlings shook their heads at the overzealousness: "And they call this SPS! They have no idea how much that idea has been distorted."* – "Dobroe utro, Sberbank!" company newsletter. 06.2011.

PAGE 85: *In an interview with The New York Times, a director of the old school shared his impressions of 5S: "At first I didn't see anything special in it. Then it hit me: they were all creating profit. No-one was messing around looking for parts, waiting to be told what to do."* Hal M. "5S for project Delivery and Baseball" // New York Times. 1972.

The Creative Class

PAGE 90: *Ten years ago, the company brought together 300,000 employees to exchange experience and provide professional advice and assistance to each other.* – https://www.collaborationjam.com/

PAGE 93: *"Encouraging innovation is one of the key objectives of the Sberbank Production System", wrote Gref in one of his monthly communiqués. "Those who innovate, our 'creative class', will be the ones who go on to greater things here."* – Letter from Gref to staff. 05.03.2009.

No More Doing The Slips!

PAGE 100: *"All our work has been taken off us and handed to the SSCs. We're all for the chop", accounts departments wailed fearfully.* – http://osberbanke.com/viewtopic.phpf=18&t=170&start=30

PAGE 100: *Fear of redundancy mingled with resentment: experience no longer counted as a measure of ability, as the centres were inundated with youngsters. "The centres have just taken on tram drivers...* – http://www.potrebclub.ru/brand-sberbank/1855/

PAGE 100: *"They're just taking people in off the street", grumbled a member of staff at the Urals centre. "Where are they supposed to find 1,500 qualified workers?"* – http://www.dengi-molodym.ru/blogs/sberbank-rossii/

PAGE 100: *In a moment of candour, a worker at Yuzhny Port wrote that she had to help out another office "at her own risk", since colleagues couldn't cope with the extra workload.* – http://osberbanke.com/viewtopic.php?f=18&t=170&start=70

PAGE 100: *"We handed over all the records to the SSCs, and now what?" was the complaint in the branches. "Total chaos when opening accounts, documents going missing all the time."* – http://osberbanke.com/viewtopic.php?f=6&t=151&start=50

PAGE 100: *It was here that Gref brought President Medvedev, impressing on him the ability of the newly kitted-out office to handle up to 2.5 million transactions per day.* "Medvedev oznakomilsya s peredovymi tekhnologiyami Sberbanka" // RIA Novosti. 29.12.2009.

The Billion-Dollar Swindle

PAGE 102: *It had been Andrei Kazmin's dream to make millions of borrowers out of the millions of depositors.* – A. Grigoriev, A Kazmin. Sberbank – eto prazdnik, kotory vsegda s toboi // Kompaniya. 09.06.2003.

PAGE 103: *One of the bank's senior auditors reported that "compromised loan portfolios" made up half of the total in some branches.* – Statement made by Oleg Chistyakov, Director of the Internal Control and Audit Department, at a 2008 bank panel.

PAGE 103: *Bank hold-ups, dishonest cash transit guards (such as those in Perm who'd snaffled 250 million roubles of Sberbank's money)...* – I. Svirskaya. Ogrableniye goda // Permsky obozrevatel'. 27.09.2009.

PAGE 103: *According to the newspaper Vedomosti...* – A. Panov, A. Baraulina, A. Nikol'sky, Y. Khutornikh. Kredit "Bezvovratny" // Vedomosti. 29.04.2008.

PAGE 103: *At a press conference, the head of Sberbank in Moscow, Maxim Poletaev, found himself having to laugh it off: "80% of arrears on retail loans, and 65% on loans to businesses are down to the criminal conduct of staff in the Lublinsky, Stromynsky and Meshchansky branches."* – "Mosheniki navredili Sberbanku na 35,4 mlrd" // Interfax. 20.01.2010.

I'll Be Making A Complaint

PAGE 112: *The Sberbank boss endeavoured to get through 300 pages a month...* M. Bakhvalova, V. Seregin. Konkurirovat' vnutri strany bessmyslenno // RBK Magazine. 2011. March.

PAGE 113: *He managed to get a temporary job at one of the 'Big Three' US car manufacturers, awkwardly wielding an impact wrench to drive in the bolts himself.* Steven Spear. Chasing The Rabbit (Russian Translation) // Institute for Complex Strategic Studies. 2010. pp. 77-79.

PAGE 113: *At the training centre, he was inducted into the art of driving in screws at different angles.* – Ibid. p. 199.

PAGE 113: *Spear's ordeal at Toyota itself only lasted six months.* – Ibid. p.224.

PAGE 113: *He'd later tell a trade journal...* – "Viktor Orlovsky: My ishchem tendentsii" // Bankovskiye tekhnologii. 2011. April.

PAGE 113: ..."*Leading companies, if they quickly break away from their competitors in a number of directions at once, become uncatchable. For the leaders, it means one thing – their strategy can't and shouldn't be based on development in one area alone, even if it is strategically the most important. (...) This approach is an unusual one for Russian business, and one that for us was neither obvious nor familiar at first.*" – Spear wrote the following: "Everyone advances over time, improving performance along various metrics such as quality, efficiency, product or service variety, workplace safety, and time to market. The problem for the pack is that the market leader achieves a certain level before everyone else and, while others close in on where the high-velocity leader was, it has darted away, still to be chased but not captured." Steven Spear. // The High Velocity Edge (Later-edition retitling of Chasing The Rabbit). McGraw-Hill. 2010. p. 2.

PAGE 115: *In Tatarstan, the book became required reading for the entire Sberbank staff.* – Internet conference with Rushan Sakhbiev // "Business online" (Tatarstan). 05.07.2010.

PAGE 119: *"If you want to know, it's not a bank at all,"* he concluded emphatically, *"it's a museum where time has stopped. The people on Facebook up in head office just don't have a clue what it's like down there."* – Anton Nosik. Sberbank – rozysk vkladov // http://blog.dp.ru/post/1556/

PAGE 119: *A debit card is blocked straight after funds are credited to an account.* – http://www.banki.ru/services/responses/bank/?responseID=3042403

PAGE 122: *Thanks to its IdeaStorm resource, Dell received around 10,000 ideas from customers (not to mention 80,000 pieces of feedback).* – http://en.community.dell.com/dellgroups/small-business/w/marketing/social-media-for-small-businessescrowdsourcing.aspx

PAGE 122: *"We invite you to hear others and be heard!" was Gref's introduction on the main page, "and we are convinced that working like this, within a 'collective intellect', is the only way of leading us to a breakthrough in the future."* – http://sberbank21.ru/intro/

PAGE 124: *"SPS got it out of us", lamented a clerk called Oksana on one of the bank forums. "Come on, work, smile like the village idiot who says hello to every Tom, Dick and Harry. But sometimes you just want to LOSE IT (sic!) at customers to get them to give their stupid questions about benefits a rest."* – http://story-online.ru/story_1378/str_4.html

Denial, Anger, Bargaining, Depression And Acceptance

PAGE 125: *The renowned US family psychologist Virginia Satir, who studied how people experience changes in their lives, called them 'foreign elements'.* – Virginia Satir. The Satir model: Family therapy and beyond // Science and Behavior Books, 1991.

PAGE 125: *The model, described by Elisabeth Kübler-Ross in her book On Death and Dying...* – Elisabeth Kübler-Ross. On Death & Dying // Macmillan, New York, 1969.

PAGE 130: *"Sberbank spends billions of roubles on bonuses to senior managers": in a country where, according to Rosstat, the average monthly salary barely exceeded 22,000 roubles, this headline from Komsomolskaya Pravda couldn't fail to attract attention.* – Komsomolskaya Pravda. 15.02.2011. Article by Maxim Brusnev.

PAGE 130: *...demanding that the bankers voluntarily waive their bonuses, at least while the economy remained in flux.* – "Molodezhnoye dvizheniye "Nashi" potrebovalo ot top-menedzherov Sberbank RF vernut' bonusy za 2008 g. v summe 933 mln rub." // Praim-TASS, 13.02.2009.

PAGE 131: *Moreover, he had every reason to delay making a quick decision on a new job, given the failures in his last.* – At that time, VimpelCom's (Beeline) management was in effect a bizarre duumvirate. After the departure of company head Alexander Izosimov, the board of directors decided to appoint not one but two CEOs – Alexander Torbakhov and Sarajevo-born Boris Nemšić. The tandem executive, nicknamed the two-headed bee, spawned doubts about its viability from the very outset.

PAGE 132: *"We have invested, and continue to invest, a huge amount of effort and money in putting together a team – we take the best people on the market, train them, cultivate top-class senior managers, and then they're bought on the open market for two to three times the amount we can afford to pay", he complained in an interview with Kommersant.* – Svetlana Dementieva. My ne gotovy k myshleniyu i k rabote v usloviyakh XXI veka // Kommersant. 03.06.2010.

PAGE 134: *"All employees have a small fixed salary, but large bonuses are available, monthly, quarterly and yearly", Gref told state television.* – Interview with Gref on TV channel Vesti 24. 11.05.2011.

Counting Shares On One Hand

PAGE 137: *It was said of the renowned US shareholder rights activist and magnate Carl Icahn that he loved two things above all else: making money, and mocking management.* – This observation of Carl Icahn comes from the billionaire's biographer, Mark Stevens, author of King Icahn: The

Biography of a Renegade Capitalist (source: Indianapolis Star, John Russell, Ted Evanoff, "Who is this guy? And does Eli Lilly need to be afraid of him?", 15.06.2008).

PAGE 138: *In 2007, the Financial Times compiled a list of the dozen most influential activist shareholders, mostly representing investment funds.* – "Most Influential activist investors" // Financial Times. 11.04.2007.

PAGE 139: *He was publicly called a crook and accused of shady dealings with Washington.* – Y. Shishkunova, A Ponamareva. Ni kapli "Transnefti" // Izvestiya. 20.05.2011.

PAGE 139: *Some complained that the Samarans weren't even invited to the November 2007 extraordinary meeting...* – I. Lipkind. Kaz'mina khotyat zasudit' // Khronograf. 26.02.2008.

PAGE 140: *Andrei Kazmin claimed to know them "by sight".* – I. Moiseev. Na tri goda sredstv ot pazmeshcheniya vpolne khvatit // Kommersant 29.06.2007.

PAGE 140: *"Igor Sechin's demeanour at the Rosneft shareholder meeting did not did not conform to his reputation as the 'grey cardinal", wrote Vedomosti.* – Yekaterina Derbilova. Debyut Sechina // Vedomosti. 02.07.2007.

PAGE 141: *For uncomfortable, chastening questions and off-putting criticisms, few compared to Navalny, an "unusual" shareholder, as Rosneft's lawyers had put it.* – http://navalny.livejournal.com/514832.html

PAGE 141: *Standing at the microphone, he painted a vivid picture: "These people sit with straight faces. A few even came here in cars with flashing lights. They are afraid. But the only way they can exist in this disgusting, corrupt system is through our silence. Don't be silent."* – http://www.youtube.com/watch?v=eqpm14I-Pys

PAGE 141: *"I have a huge number of issues with Gref. We have quite an aggressive correspondence. But his large salary doesn't bother me particularly. It's an average salary, which compares to similar salaries in similar banks. That's not a problem"*, Navalny told *Ekho Moskvy*. – Ekho Mosky broadcast // http://echo.msk.ru/programs/dayaftertomorrow/676295-echo/

PAGE 142: *"The workers are of course not to blame for anything, but the bank can't simply write off loans on one official's say so",* was how Navalny explained his position. – http://navalny.livejournal.com/375165.html

PAGE 142: ..."*which clearly wouldn't bring in substantial profits in the foreseeable future."* – Ekho Mosky broadcast // http://echo.msk.ru/programs/dayaftertomorrow/676295-echo/

PAGE 143: *Navalny expressed the essence of his position succinctly: "I believe that I am the bank. However, the bank believes that I'm not."* – http://navalny.livejournal.com/362883.html?thread=6722691#t6722691

PAGE 143: *"Gref has shown himself to be a good man",* Alexei wrote on his blog. – http://navalny.livejournal.com/559361.html

PAGE 144: *Anton Danilov-Danilyan, in charge of relations between the bank and minority shareholders, had proudly reported at the annual meeting that the notorious activist was acting unusually "amicably and constructively".* – Sberbank shareholder AGM 03.06.2011 // – http://sberbank.ru/moscow/ru/investor_relations/shareholders_meetings/annualmeeting/

PAGE 144: *Back in 2006, while Kazmin was still in charge, non-resident stockholding had accounted for at least 20% of the total.* – "Dolya inostrannykh aktsionerov v kapitale Sberbanka sostavlyaet okolo 20%" // RIA Novosti. 05.04.2006.

PAGE 145: *"I do not consider myself a crook. I don't feel I should I apologise for anything or to anyone and am prepared to state my case on any question that may be of interest to you",* Gref retorted at one meeting after an attack from the hall. – Sberbank shareholder AGM 03.06.2011 // – http://sberbank.ru/

moscow/ru/investor_relations/shareholders_meetings/annualmeeting/

PAGE 145: *The Economist estimated that $100 invested in Sberbank in 2002 would yield $3,722 for the fortunate shareholder by 2012.* – Some time later, the same publication, which had previously been notably unsympathetic towards Russia, published a complimentary article on Sberbank: "Abacus to ATM: The transformation of Sberbank into a modern financial institution", 23.06.2012.

PAGE 145: *Moreover, according to 2011 analysis conducted by Boston Consulting Group, the Russian state bank was the second most successful bank in the world for returns on assets...* – T. Voronova. BCG: Sberbank – vtoroi v mire po dokhodnosti // Vedomosti. 07.06.2012.

Spare People

PAGE 148: *"By making Sberbank better, we have the chance to improve the lives of 270,000 people," wrote Gref in spring 2009 in his monthly letter to staff.* – Letter from Gref to staff. 10.04.2009.

PAGE 149: *But the shake-up didn't seriously affect staff numbers – they decreased by 2% (in all, 4,028 people).* – Sberbank annual report for 2000. p. 38.

PAGE 149: *It was bloated even by Soviet standards: in 1988, in the whole of the USSR, including the non-Russian republics, Sberbank employed 248,000 people.* – Sberbank v postsovetskoi Rossii // http://www.memoid.ru/node/Sberbank_v_postsovetskoj_Rossii

PAGE 150: *Management was forced to abandon the idea, despite having already signed off on the redundancies of 5,000 workers.* – "AvtoVAZ sokrashchaet pochti pyat' tysyach chelovek" // RIA Novosti. 14.09.2009.

PAGE 151: *Toyota, Matsushita and the other great corporations in the Land of the Rising Sun didn't lay anyone off (the sacking of 2,146 Toyota workers during an acute sales crisis and severe money shortage in 1950 led to a two-month strike, after which company president Kiichiro Toyoda resigned)...* – Daniel T. Jones and James P. Womack. Lean Thinking: Banish Waste and Create Wealth in Your Corporation (Russian translation) // Alpina Business Books. 2004. p. 294.

PAGE 152: *He was deeply taken with the ideas of W. Edwards Deming, the father of Japan's quality revolution. One of his commandments had particular resonance for Fidelman: employees are to blame for no more than 2% of a company's problems; the other 98% are failures of the system.* – Fidelman's commitment to this principle was evident in his preface to the Russian edition of Henry R. Neave's The Deming Dimension: "Deming's 98/2 formula inevitably leads us to the fundamental conclusion that punishing people is not only pointless, but actually detrimental to the company."

PAGE 152: *Ten years earlier, Microsoft boss Bill Gates had questioned the need for banks to exist in their present form at all.* – James Mackintosh. The bank is dead... // Financial Times. 04.10.2000.

PAGE 152: *The Economist once suggested to its readers that if competitive advantages took the form of objects that could be dropped on one's foot, then they strongly advised revising one's business strategy.* – The magazine was quoting Kjell Nordström and Jonas Ridderstråle in Funky Business: Capital Makes Talent Dance // FT Press. 2000.

PAGE 153: *As services went online – according to IT director Viktor Orlovsky, this applied to 90% of services at some Western banks, and Sberbank was moving in a similar direction – people and premises were destined to become burdensome.* – A. Levashov. Sberbank postroil MegaTSOD za $1,2 mlrd // Cnews.ru. 11.12.2011.

PAGE 155: *...(one of them, Antoin Murphy, came to the conclusion that in a country as small as Ireland, whose population at that time was around three million people, life could go on just fine* *without banks).* – Antoin Murphy. Money in an Economy without Banks: The Case of Ireland // The Manchester School, 1978. pp. 41–50.

PAGE 155: *Approximately 400,000 bank workers in Brazil, acting through their union, demanded salary increases from the National Banking Federation (Fedraban).* – Brazil bank workers to strike nationwide over pay // Reuters. 28.09.2010.

PAGE 155: *Staff in Israeli banks frequently went on strike to demand payment of bonuses and the renewal of collective agreements without change of conditions.* – Vseobshchaya zabastovka vo imya interesov banka // Israelinfo.ru (with a link to Israeli news portal NRG-Maariv). 14.04. 2008.

PAGE 155: *The only noted attempt to create an independent organisation was undertaken in 2007 by a former Citibank branch employee, Ilya Strokov.* – The Ilya Strokov case was a subject of discussion on internet forums at the time (http://govorim-vsem.ru/viewtopic.php?f=1&t=29244). In addition, Strokov wrote a book with Galina Yenyutina titled "Kak ne okazat'sya obmanutym i uvolenym" ("How Not To Be Deceived and Fired") // ANO: Center For Social & Labor Rights, 2008.

An Unlucky Number

PAGE 158: *In the British capital, there was one bank branch for every 5,300 people; in the Russian capital, it was one for every 3,520.* – N. Biyanova. Dom bankira // SmartMoney (Russia). 10.11.2008.

PAGE 161: *"The city's budget is second only to that of New York", announced Mayor Luzhkov proudly in autumn 2007.* – "Byudzhet Moskvy prevysit k 2012 godu nyneshny byudzhet New Yorka // ITAR-TASS. 21.09.2007.

PAGE 161: *Sberbank's attempts to claw back its position with specialised express lending were unsuccessful.* – Y. Berezanskaya, N Mazurin. Pod Grefom // Forbes Russia. 03.04.2008.

PAGE 162: *...in a farewell interview, when his move to Russian Post was already sealed, he listed it among his ten greatest achievements at the bank.* – D. Simonov, O. Kameneva, V Karpinskaya. Itogi s Andreem Kaz'minym // Pryamye investitsii. 2007. November.

Out Of The Blue

PAGE 167: *Finance minister Alexei Kudrin described Russia as "an island of stability" in a global ocean of liquidity problems.* – T. Konishcheva. Krizis v Davose: Aleksei Kudrin ob"yasnil inostrannomu biznesu, pochemu Rossiya okazalas' ostrovom stabil'nosti // Rossiyskaya Gazeta. 21.01.2008.

PAGE 168: *"It's awful when a situation appears out of the blue", Gref said later of that calamitous autumn.* – Gref's appearance on "Pozner", Channel One (Russia). 15.06.2009.

PAGE 170: *"We need to be ready for a three-year crisis", Gref prophesied at a meeting with journalists in early February 2009.* – ITAR-TASS. 03.02.2009.

PAGE 170: *To be on the safe side, Sberbank borrowed 0.5 trillion roubles from the Central Bank...* – N Biyanova. Minfin prosporil 56,5 mlrd rub. // Kommersant. 21.06.2010.

PAGE 171: *"Banks are beginning to shed real estate, as property owners themselves are doing. I think this will create an additional wave that will sweep the market. Along with the crises in banking, one wave may overlap the next, and I think the situation will become very serious", warned the expert.* – Alexei Chuvin's appearance at an Adam Smith Conference // Nedvizhimost' v Rossii. 02.06.2009. (http://slon.ru/economics/aleksey_chuvin_sberbank_situaciey_zloupotreblyayut-43104.xhtml)

PAGE 171: *"We would have reprimanded him for that, not fired him", stated Gref publicly.* – Gref's appearance on "Pozner", Channel One (Russia). 15.06.2009.

PAGE 173: *The 2.25 billion roubles that MAIR had borrowed from Sberbank to carry out technical refits at its plants...* – Alexander Vorobiev. "Staks" narabotal na stat'yu // Kommersant (Rostov) 05.08.2009.

PAGE 173: *...but was then "attacked by authorities of the Russian Federation, as a result of which [the group] was deprived of a large part of its assets".* – http://www.mair.ru/about.php

Kicking Clients When They're Down?

PAGE 177: *After shops and poultry plants, the businessman planned to throw up skyscrapers in Siberia's cities.* – The businessmen maintained his plans for high-rise construction: "We have poultry farms, shops, hypermarkets, a bank, a construction company – we will build skyscrapers", he told the magazine Delovoi Kvartal (Krasnoyarsk) // O. Ryabova. Aleksei Podsokhin, kinoprodyuser s ptitsefabriki. 21.03.2011.

PAGE 177: *In 2007, Oleg Bolychev, founder of the modest Kaliningrad-based retailer Vester, promised to increase his supermarket revenue 12 times in 18 months to $2.2 billion.* – Y. Nikitina. Bol'shoye iz malen'kogo // SmartMoney (Russia). 13.8.2007.

PAGE 177: *In the same pre-crisis year, former CEO of retail chain Mosmart Eric Blondeau was confidently giving estimates for the construction of a federation-wide, multiformat chain to compete with French-owned Auchan.* – P. Kulikov. Raznostoronny riteiler // Sekret firmy. 20.02.2007.

PAGE 179: *In spring 2011, financial recovery procedures were instigated against the company.* – N. Kopeichenko. "Dikaya orkhideya" priznana bankrotom // RBK Daily. 27.07.2011.

PAGE 181: *"The majority of large business owners have known me personally for a long time," said Khachaturyants in an interview with Vedomosti.* – G. Gubeidullina, M. Rykova. Chego nas boyat'sya – my ne reidery // Vedomosti. 11.11.2009.

PAGE 183: *In spring 2011, the investigative eye of weekly publication The New Times, renowned for its bold exposés of government corruption, turned on Khachaturyants.* – Ilya Barabanov. Reidersky zakhvat. Kak gosudarstvo zakhvatyvaet "Energomash" // The New Times. 14.03.2011.

PAGE 184: *The magazine was run by the rather eccentric Yevgenia Albats, grande dame of the free Russian press, whose doctorate from Harvard did not temper scathing judgements of her fellow journalists.* – Albats had once demanded that a journalist from the online Moscow News, Anna Harutyunyan, give up journalism. The dialogue that took place on Harutyunyan's blog after Albats's "Polny Al'bats" show on Ekho Moskvy, itself a rather haughty affair broadcast on 22.10.2006, became a subject of much discussion on the internet.

PAGE 184: *...(the same prison that had once briefly held the writer Oscar Wilde, albeit on very different charges).* – In 1895, the Irish writer was accused of sodomy. He was first held at Pentonville Prison, before being transferred to another London jail (Wandsworth).

More Than A Bank

PAGE 188: *However, this share block, bought for $1.5 billion, soon ended up in the hands of the oligarch's creditors...* – D. Belikov, M. Cherkasova. Oleg Deripaska lishilsya zapchastei // Kommersant. 06.10.2008.

PAGE 189: *"Opel is solvent – the crisis is at General Motors", affirmed the chairman of the Opel works council, Klaus Franz.* – Opel potrebuyutsya gosgarantii na kredit pochti v 2 mlrd yevro // RIA Novosti. 19.11.2008.

PAGE 189: *To cover 'worst-case scenario' losses, the company needed to borrow up to €1.8 billion...* – Sueddeutsche Zeitung, Von C. Gammelin, M. Koch, H. Schwarz u. G. Bohsem. Kein VEB Opel. 19.11.2008.

PAGE 189: *Gref believed that this Eurasian giant would be producing six million cars per year in the space of five years.* – Gref prigovoril "AvtoVAZ" // Interfax. 16.06.2009.

PAGE 190: *...it had sold 2.2 million cars...* – GM annual report for 2007. p. 8. (http://bigthreeauto.procon.org/sourcefiles/ GM_AR_2007.pdf)

PAGE 192: *In 2010, for example, the company spent more than $9.5 billion on new development projects...* – Volkswagen annual report for 2010. p. 186. (http://www.volkswagenag. com/content/vwcorp/content/en/misc/pdf-dummies.bin. html/downloadfilelist/downloadfile/downloadfile_14/file/ Y_2010_e.pdf)

PAGE 192: *...three times more than GM.* – GM annual report for 2010. p. 147. (https://materials.proxyvote.com/ Approved/37045V/20110408/AR_87685/images/General_ Motors-AR2010.pdf)

PAGE 193: *AutoVAZ's annual reports...* – AvtoVAZ annual report. p. 85. (http://www.ladaauto.ru/images/annuals/ annual_2010.pdf)

PAGE 195: *Vladimir Putin rushed to call the deal one of the first steps towards "real integration with the European economy".* – From a report of Putin's meeting with delegates from the sixth Valdai International Discussion Club (http:// government.ru/docs/4990/print/)

PAGE 196: *He believed, for example, that by studying the characteristics of local markets, the bank could apply the microfinancing experiences of Nobel laureate Muhammad Yunus, founder of the renowned Grameen Bank, which provided small loans (no more than $100 on average) to poor Bangladeshi farmers.* – Y. Chaikina, I. Moiseev. German Gref zagnul kreditnuyu liniyu // Kommersant. 05.03.2008.

PAGE 196: *"We could be earning much more money from these investments," he observed during an interview with one of Russia's main TV stations. "It's quite a complex and risky purchase, unprecedented in Russian history, and one which for us is clearly not motivated by profit. It's first and foremost an attempt to help restructure our car industry."* – Gref's appearance on "Pozner", Channel One (Russia). 15.06.2009.

PAGE 197: *"If that doesn't happen, we've wasted our time," he told a Sochi economic forum in September.* – Gref: Sdelka po priobreteniyu Opel oznachaet import tekhnologii v Rossiyu // RIA Novosti. 19.09.2009.

PAGE 197: *At the end of October, GM head Fritz Henderson told The Financial Times that they were looking to complete the necessary paperwork over the coming days and close the deal by December.* – John Reed, Daniel Schäfer. GM delays Opel sale until November // Financial Times. 23.09.2009.

PAGE 197: *By June, The Times was reporting, with some dismay, that "Sberbank, Vauxhall's new part-owner, is the Big Daddy of Russian banks, practically an extension of the state budget in implementing the Kremlin's industrial policies."* – Tony Halpin. Vauxhall line to Kremlin // Times. 02.06.2009.

PAGE 198: *Wolfgang Porsche, chairman of the eponymous car manufacturer's supervisory board, decried the Americans' decision as a dirty trick.* – http://suite101.de/article/ueberblick-stimmen-zum-verbleib-von-opel-bei-gm-a64336

PAGE 198: *The press reported anonymous sources quoting €13 million...* – N. Starostina. Sberbank poluchil za Opel // RBK Daily. 24.06.2010.

PAGE 198: *"I invested a fair amount of my own time in this", Gref reminded shareholders.* – N. Starostina. Sberbank poluchil za Opel // RBK Daily. 24.06.2010.

Buying Time

PAGE 200: *...one of which was titled "Ruben Vardanian at the helm of Troika Dialog".* – T. Antropova. Lidery formiruyutsya na minnom pole // Kompaniya. 19.07.2004.

PAGE 201: *Ruben even had talks with Andrei Kazmin, though evidently made little headway.* – N. Mazurina, T. Lysova. Net konflikta, prosto yest' dve razniye modeli // Vedomosti. 09.04.2002.

PAGE 207: *"We resolve any issues within a day, two at most," Ruben told Kommersant.* – Y. Golikova. Ne nado putat' turizm s emigratsiyei // Kommersant. 30.05.2011.

PAGE 209: *"Even a year ago, we wouldn't have been able to carry out a deal like this because of our complete mental unreadiness," Gref told Kommersant. "To be honest, this is another big test for us."* – Y. Golikova. Sposobnost' "Troika" generirovat' pribyl' byla predmetom diskussii // Kommersant. 30.05.2011.

Isn't It Just Us?

PAGE 212: *Even Kazmin had come out in support of the government as it was defending its restriction of the activities of foreign banks during negotiations on accession to the WTO, agreeing to permit subsidiaries to operate only under the strict control of the Russian banking regulator.* – Dolya inostrannykh aktsionerov v kapitale Sberbanka sostavlyaet okolo 20% // RIA Novosti. 05.04.2006.

PAGE 212: *In 2002, there were 27 such banks in the country, controlling 5.4% of Russian financial assets.* – Effektivnaya Rossiya. Proizvoditel'nost' kak fundament rosta. Section of " Proizvoditel'nost' roznichnogo bankovskogo sektora" // V. Klintsov, D. Popov, D. Tafintsev, I. Shvakman // McKinsey Global Institute. 2009. April. P 106.

PAGE 215: *In spring 2010, Sberbank joined British market research agency Millward Brown's list of the 100 most valuable international brands, and for the next two years rubbed shoulders with Wall Street stalwarts such as Citigroup, J.P. Morgan Chase and Goldman Sachs.* – In the Millward Brown Optimor top-100 published in May 2011, Sberbank ranked 99th ($8.5 billion); within a year, it had risen to 74th ($10.6 billion).

PAGE 215: *Andrei Kazmin had been sceptical of going beyond the boundaries of the former Soviet Union.* – D. Simonov, O. Kameneva, V Karpinskaya. Itogi s Andreem Kaz'minym // Pryamye investitsii. 2007. November.

PAGE 215: *In the long term – in 20 to 30 years – Gref hoped to increase revenue generated from overseas assets to 50% of the bank's total.* – "Gref nadeyetsya, chto cherez 20-30 let Sberbank budet imet' 50% dokhodov ot zarubezhnykh aktivov" // Praim. 01.06.2012.

PAGE 218: *In an interview he later gave to Die Presse in Vienna, he steered clear of any bold statements.* – Eduard Steiner. Sberbank-Chef: Europa liegt uns näher als China // Die Presse. 11.09.2011.

PAGE 219: *...over the last 15 years, after a couple of crises, their numbers decreased by two and half times, and this decline slowly continued.* – In his book Building Capitalism: The Transformation of the Former Soviet Bloc, Anders Åslund provides figures which show that by 1994, more than 2,500 banks were registered in Russia. According to data from the Central Bank of the Russian Federation, 908 banks were active in June 2012.

Dear Reader,

Thank you for purchasing this book.

We at Glagoslav Publications are glad to welcome you, and hope that you find our books to be a source of knowledge and inspiration.

We want to show the beauty and depth of the Slavic region to everyone looking to expand their horizon and learn something new about different cultures, different people, and we believe that with this book we have managed to do just that.

Now that you've got to know us, we want to get to know you. We value communication with our readers and want to hear from you! We offer several options:

- Join our Book Club on Goodreads, Library Thing and Shelfari, and receive special offers and information about our giveaways;

- Share your opinion about our books on Amazon, Barnes & Noble, Waterstones and other bookstores;

- Join us on Facebook and Twitter for updates on our publications and news about our authors;

- Visit our site www.glagoslav.com to check out our Catalogue and subscribe to our Newsletter.

Glagoslav Publications is getting ready to release a new collection and planning some interesting surprises – stay with us to find out!

Glagoslav Publications
Office 36, 88-90 Hatton Garden
EC1N 8PN London, UK
Tel: + 44 (0) 20 32 86 99 82
Email: contact@glagoslav.com

Glagoslav Publications Catalogue

- *The Time of Women* by Elena Chizhova
- *Sin* by Zakhar Prilepin
- *Hardly Ever Otherwise* by Maria Matios
- *The Lost Button* by Irene Rozdobudko
- *Khatyn* by Ales Adamovich
- *Christened with Crosses* by Eduard Kochergin
- *The Vital Needs of the Dead* by Igor Sakhnovsky
- *METRO 2033* (Dutch Edition) by Dmitry Glukhovsky
- *METRO 2034* (Dutch Edition) by Dmitry Glukhovsky
- *A Poet and Bin Laden* by Hamid Ismailov
- *Asystole* by Oleg Pavlov
- *Kobzar* by Taras Shevchenko
- *White Shanghai* by Elvira Baryakina
- *The Stone Bridge* by Alexander Terekhov
- *King Stakh's Wild Hunt* by Uladzimir Karatkevich
- *Depeche Mode* by Serhii Zhadan
- *Saraband Sarah's Band* by Larysa Denysenko
- *Herstories*, An Anthology of New Ukrainian Women Prose Writers
- *Watching The Russians* (Dutch Edition) by Maria Konyukova
- *The Hawks of Peace* by Dmitry Rogozin
- *The Grand Slam and Other Stories* (Dutch Edition) by Leonid Andreev

More coming soon…

www.ingramcontent.com/pod-product-compliance
Lightning Source LLC
Chambersburg PA
CBHW020903080526
44589CB00011B/426